My Life Before t... YO-EKS-124
The Pre-Posthumous Stories and Poetry of
Robert Henry Walz

by
Robert Henry Walz

Printed Edition
ISBN 978-1-480177-11-6

PUBLISHED BY:
Judy Fitzpatrick

My Life Before the Bottle Went Dry
The Pre-Posthumous Stories and Poetry of
Robert Henry Walz

Cover Design: Val Edward Simone

My Life Before the Bottle Went Dry - The Pre-Posthumous Stories and Poems of Robert Henry Walz is a work containing both fiction and non-fiction. The author acknowledges the trademarked status and trademark owners of various products referenced in the portions of fiction, which have been used without permission. The publication/use of these trademarks is not authorized, associated with, or sponsored by the trademark owners.

i

About the Author

Robert Henry Walz

Robert Henry Walz, known affectionately as *Walzie*, *Bob*, *Copabob*, and a myriad of other suitable nicknames, was born in Vancouver, Washington on September 2, 1947, to a life constantly filled with adventure.

He first attended BYU then was a U.S. Marine who served in Vietnam. After his military service was completed, Bob attended and graduated from the University of Washington with a degree in International Relations and English Literature.

As an avid collector of art and memorabilia of all types, he put his fascination to good purpose, opening an art gallery in Seattle's Capitol Hill area in the 1980s.

Sometime during the early 1990s, Bob moved to Boulder, CO, and began his work in public relations. He also began his tour and travel business. Over the many years that followed, he guided adventure and travel safaris to over seven different international destinations. Bob was enthusiastic about Ernest Hemingway and all things Cuban. He was especially fond of the tours he guided to Cuba, in particular, the trip with his Mother, Pat, on her 80th birthday.

Bob returned to Vancouver and his childhood home in 2005, to be a loving caregiver to his parents in their last years. During this period, he developed his amazing love of art into creating haunting and inspiring assemblages of xxx art, utilizing his mastery of words and images. He was also a big lover of literature.

Bob was a prolific writer of *Letters to the Editor* which were often published in numerous publications. Most of all though he loved to tell a good story. Never allowing the truth to get in his way, he took his audience on a majestic and rousing journey.

Bob made friends wherever he went and will be forever missed by many. He passed away quietly in his sleep on November 9, 2011, his life's wondrous journey finally completed.

Dedication:
To family, friends, and supporters.

With Special Thanks To:
Bud and Pat - Parents
Judy Fitzpatrick - Sister
James Fitzpatrick - Nephew
Michelle Walbert - Transcriptionist

<u>Editors</u>
Judy Fitzpatrick
*
Val Edward Simone
Morningside Publishing, LLC
*
Judith Sansweet
Website: www.proofreadnz.co.nz
Email: judith@proofreadnz.co.nz

FOREWORD

On several occasions, Robert and I discussed how this book was to be developed and completed. He made it very clear to me that he had no intention whatsoever of reconstructing the story of his *wild child* life. "Everyone who knows me well already knows those stories," he said plainly and simply.

He wanted to briefly highlight certain areas of his past that he felt were important to illustrate not where he had come from, but why he ended up where he did.

Therefore, much of his *wild child* youth will not be addressed here, except, perhaps in some passing comment intended to illustrate some other point. What Robert intended was to represent only those times, places, events, and certain people who had the most profound effect on him over the years — the driving forces that necessarily brought him to the end game.

Robert gave me several leather-bound books of his last journeys. He sent me every electronic file imaginable containing his thoughts, hopes, dreams, and wishes. And, yes, he also sent me all accounts of his fears, perversions, cautions, and terrors as well.

The only restriction placed upon me in preparing this book was his desire for me to only reprint such accounts as were necessary to tell the stories he wanted told…and those to be held tightly within a very restrained context. I have tried to the best of my abilities to do just that.

To the many of you who claim to know Robert well, you already know that truth and precision were not necessary prerequisites to telling a good story. Many of his *stories* were based on his audience and what he thought best as to how to effectively entertain them. The simple stories often morphed into epics as required to hold his audience's attention and interest. That is what we loved most about Robert; he was, in the absence of all else, a true master storyteller.

He instructed me to only share glimpses of his past that were necessary to explore the larger story of his true desires. Therefore, you will not find detailed accounts of any specific time in his earlier life. What you shall see is only that which he deemed necessary to set the stage for his greatest audience of all — you.

He was particularly interested in telling the story of his last true exploit to Afghanistan. Much of the narrative portion of this book, therefore, is dedicated to that journey at his specific and insistent request.

I cannot possibly certify that any part of the story is true or even remotely accurate. I have tried to the best of my abilities to keep faithful to his voice. Much of what I received was incoherent at best. There are passages, nevertheless, which I feel offer brilliant lucidity and rich insight to the workings of his brain during those end times. I have tried, as best as I was able, to reproduce his thoughts without inserting any of my own into his work. My effort to rejoin all the disjointed paragraphs and phrases, disconnected stray thoughts, and ramblings was only accomplished after several readings during which I tried to ascertain his original intent, and after many reviews of the extensive notes of our conversations regarding all his own notes and writings. I think, for the most part, working together as we did, we were able to reconstruct much of what was his original intent. However, if there are any errors, I must accept them as mine, for he was never able to finish the notes, and I, thusly, was lacking specific knowledge of the events in their totality.

The humor and wit, of course, is all Robert. The candidness is all Robert as well.

The poetry contained herein, with the structure or lack of structure as you'll see, was faithfully reproduced. Robert always said that his poetry style was directly influenced by his favorite poet, Charles Bukowski. His style, mostly his own, was necessarily developed in the spirit of his admiration of Mr. Bukowski's own abstract construction. I have, for the most part, reproduced his poetry exactly as Robert wrote it, lacking punctuation, stanza construction, etc. The way I see it, this is what Robert saw in his head. Who, therefore, am I to change it?

The children's short stories, however, required extensive rewriting due to the incoherency of his sentences and disjointed wording. The nature of the stories were faithfully maintained, but, once again, the paragraph structure, if there was any structure to them at all, was woefully inadequate: so much so as to render the stories nearly indecipherable. Thankfully, though, Robert and I went through each story in depth, and I was able to take good note of his intentions. The stories themselves are true *Bobisms*. They are true treasures.

To say that Robert was a unique spirit would

not do him justice. Those of you who knew him also, know what I'm saying. My life has been so enriched just by knowing him. Our nearly daily five to six telephone conversations were each in their own way unique as well. His patented "Goodbye" at each conversation's end, spat out in mock disgust, I shall never forget.

Robert was a people person. He loved people and it showed in almost every encounter. His Cuban friends and partners speak of him to this day as if he were still alive and about to make another appearance on their fair shores. He touched many lives in such a wonderful manner and depth that many of us will never ever forget him. I count myself among the very fortunate to have his trust and faith to reproduce this book on his behalf. I hope you enjoy reading it and experience the incredible mind of the man known affectionately to many of us simply as CopaBob.

Val Edward Simone,
Author, editor, publisher, friend,
confidant and true believer
Morningside Publishing, LLC

A Special Memory

TOMA CHOCOLATE... PAY WHAT YOU OWE

The Adventures and Misadventures of Bob Walz and his love for Cuba.

By Cesar Gomez Chacon

The great Nat King Cole back in the late 50s used to repeat over and over again in the Tropicana, the most famous Cabaret of the Caribbean, the chorus of *El Bodeguero*: "tooomaaaaa chocolate, paga lo que debes....." Nat used to travel to Batista's Havana to delight with his music and his voice the hundreds of well-heeled Americans and Cubans who enjoyed a night in one of the best places of the world.

Robert (Bob) Henry Walz, from Boulder, Colorado, arrived to Havana almost four decades after Nat. He was a mix of Hemingway and Indiana Jones. He had Hemingway's white beard and his devotion for Cuba, and from Indiana Jones that patriotic and adventurous spirit. As a patriot, he went to Vietnam to fight for his country. As an adventurer, he came to Cuba without the permission from his government.

He appeared one day in 1994, driven by a curious way of enjoying life.

Bob moved from project to project, He met, for example, a group of poor children who loved football and there sprang an amazing idea. First, he contacted a famous football team and then he organized an exhibition game. Then, with his indisputable charisma, *embullaba* in good Cuban language, he would 'convince' (in English) a movie star, or a famous musician to follow his cause as a special attraction to the media.

These personalities, interested in the perennial stories of princes and paupers and assuring a good promotion for themselves invited some other Good Samaritans to join the project, even the Mayor of a town who did not want to stay behind.

The project favoured everyone. The children made their dream come true; for one day with sneakers and autographed balls, and with some luck, the municipal office would donate the money to build a low budget football court.

The stars and athletes shined a little more and the press had a good story and paid for it. Bob got what he wanted: besides the money to go on, the immense satisfaction of doing good for others and seeing himself on television and in the newspapers — something that he enjoyed a lot.

That was his resume when he came to Cuba for the first time: a file containing articles from some American newspapers talking about all those projects that he had successfully completed. His first proposal was to organize a marathon race in the city of Havana in which American citizens could participate including a sport star just to gain more popularity. He himself organized the trip and paid for the expenses of the project. He just needed the authorization and organizational logistics provided by the Cuban authorities.

In a couple of days he received the permission from the INDER (Cuban National Institute of Sports and Recreation) with its leader's concerns about whether he was capable of fulfilling his promises, because doing this, he was going to defy the US restrictions of the embargo against the island.

Bob Walz reaffirmed his decision. He did not seem to mind the risks that he was already taking (although the Cuban authorities explained them all) the fact that he traveled to the island without the permission of the US Treasury Department could bring him serious problems with his government. Bob also had rejected the option offered by the Cuban Immigration of not stamping the entrance visa to Cuba on the passport of someone who so requested.

Several weeks later, he almost did everything he had promised: About forty Americans of both sexes between 14 and 80 years of age disembarked from the plane that brought them to Cuba from Mexico City because at that time direct flights from US to Cuba were not allowed.

It is true that the only 'star' that Bob was able to bring to the island was a Mexican marathon runner that lived in the U.S. and whose greatest moments were already "ancient history." Some journalists and reporters came to Havana to cover the event.

The race all along the Malecon, a beautiful 5-mile sea-front avenue and the participation of important Cuban track and field champions was a success. The program of several days organized by the INDER took the visitors to places linked to Hemingway's life in Cuba and the Americans also had a Marlin fishing day.

Everything worked wonderfully and the Americans publicly thanked 'Mr. Walz' for the beautiful adventure that they had just lived, and he was happy to grant all the interviews that were asked by the reporters of both countries.

This was the way he started his relationship with Cuba. He traveled once every two months as a host of other groups interested in tasting the forbidden 'chocolate' like playing baseball with Cubans, fishing where Hemingway used to fish, smoking a cigar in the Cigar's Festivals and even share a table with Fidel Castro.

That boy, hidden in an old gringo custom, showed as his biggest prize his passport, in which he had a vast collection of entry visa stamps to Cuba. "Are you crazy? Take care, Bob." This sentence was said by every friend he found in Havana; his answer was always the same: some joke, a wink and a smile in his childish face.

And then it happened: one morning, a group of his Cuban friends received a letter from a Bob that we didn't know; he was terrified, He told us he had been called from Washington to be questioned about his trips to Cuba. Then two men came to his house in Boulder and handed him a letter from the Treasury Department (he attached a copy). In it he had been warned that for "violating the embargo" and for "trading with the enemy," he could be fined up to $55,000 and could expect to spend ten years in prison.

He told us he was forced to fill out a questionnaire with dozens of questions about his activities and contacts in Cuba. He also knew the government had been poking in his bank account and he'd been threatened that it would be frozen.

Robert Henry Walz, the most common of Americans, did not know what to do to protect his rights, violated by the same government that once he defended in Vietnam.

Months passed before he returned to Havana, and in a very respectful way he eluded each and every one of our questions about the letter and the threats. We never knew exactly how this 'incident' ended; the truth is that Bob did not give up his good relations with the island.

For this reason, in 1996, he founded and presided over the company, Last Frontier Expeditions, which organized and brought groups of Americans to Cuba. Check the Internet (www.hemingwaytoursandsafaries.com)[1] to see his vast and prolific activities and what is said about these expeditions by the ones who participated in them.

Robert showed thousands of Americans a friendly country that was very near, a very polite and cultured people they never would have known in any other way. Bob's friends say today that he never subordinated himself to the rules of the embargo.

One time he took the famous photographer Roberto Salas and his father, the great Osvaldo Salas, along with some of their work, depicting Cuba and its revolution, to New York. The exhibition had to be removed because there was a bomb threat. Bob used to talk about this as one would speak about a safari in Africa.

On another occasion, traveling by plane to Havana, Bob explained in detail all his projects with Cuba to the person that was seated next to him; this man turn pale and didn't let Bob finish; he identified himself as a high-ranking officer of the Interest Section of The United States of America in Havana, and set a date for Bob to meet with him the following day.

Bob obviously never went to the meeting, and kept returning to Cuba — no matter what the consequences.

---

[1] - The website has since been removed.

In recent times, our paths didn't cross, and I hardly heard from him, We say hello to each other through e-mail, the last time took place in October 2011; he wrote with enthusiasm about the publication of a poetry book, a new trip to Cuba, and his desire to see me in order to remember together those days of his first visit 20 years ago. He used to make with me a joke, telling that I have been the one and only communist that he had met in Havana.

On November 9th I received an unexpected communication from one of his closest friends. "Bob Walz died a couple of days ago," said the brief e-mail. Through other messages from relatives and friends, I knew about the long and progressive deterioration of his health. Meanwhile, he continued developing new projects of affection and love in some other "dark corners of the planet."

Two days ago, I received an invitation from his family to participate in an event dedicated to his memory on January 15, 2011. In the letter of the invitation there was a photograph of Bob sitting by the sea in the Club Havana of Cuba. A better place could not have been chosen.

I also want to remember him like this, with that kind look and his jokes as well. His mother, an outstanding and very clever woman who had been a war reporter in Vietnam, came to Cuba in one of the trips organized by Bob. She said: "Bob is a free man with a rebel soul, but very tender."

In these days, when from Washington and

Miami people who feel hate and revenge against Cuba are talking louder, the life of Bob Walz, the most common of the Americans, stands up as the better answer ever given.

He planted hundreds of trees of friendship and trust between the Cuban and the American people. Cuba reciprocated with love, but Washington paid him with threats and terror. Still, Bob kept dreaming and doing good and laughing about it. Maybe the best of his jokes, the one that we never understood was his determination to listen constantly to that famous song popularized by old Nat in the Tropicana: "Drink chocolate ... pay what you owe."

The Beginning, the End, or Someplace In-Between

I have, it seems, always lived my life somewhere between quotation marks.

Some might call them restrictive or life-limiting. But those little marks provided me with a clear delineation for whatever I might have described as my life.

Without their guidance to hold me fast between the breadth of those ink spots, I might never have lived at all.

During my life, I gave it my best shot by draining dry every bottle I ever met, and I have well known many — this was my inspired attempt to discover which bottle held the last vestiges of my life.

It was a search that would take me a tumultuous lifetime to complete. With every bottle I drained, as my single eye peered into its bottom, I tried to find exactly who I was. What I discovered was beyond any expectation.

I will not spend any time here trying to regurgitate my 'wild child' youth. Those who know me well know that all that preceded my later days were only precursors of what my life would turn out to be. I see now, only after years of introspective thought and consideration, tears, and terror, that the events born during such an undisciplined youth were merely tracks in the sea of shifting desert sand, following my damaged soul only farther into the black heart of the desolate wilderness.

Those of you who spent those 'character-building' days with me have all the memories you can stand. I shall leave them all to you to share or to hide as you see fit.

Cuba the 'Forbidden Fruit'

It has been said that "the Rooster takes credit for the Sunrise," because lacking his urging, the sun does not have sense enough to rise on its own.

The urging I received from the universe was loud, inspiring, and unmistakable. "Come to Cuba," the voice beckoned. "Come to the land of the 'forbidden fruit'."

Hearing the term 'forbidden fruit' screaming in my brain was all I needed. The quotation marks were meant for me specifically, and I eagerly hearkened to their shrill call.

As I see it now, through their shouting and bellowing, the higher dwellers of the universe, in that moment, became solely responsible for what befell me during all those following years.

It was during those times, though, that I adopted one simple rule to live by: "It's never too early for a party."

I first heard about Cuba as a boy in Vancouver, WA. I had walked home from school on October 13, 1962 with Roger Ehle. My dad, a prominent doctor, was home unusually early. It was the first time I had seen him at home before the professional, German-Catholic mandated work hour of 6:00 p.m. I hung my raincoat in the kitchen closet and watched as Dad and Mom sat, affixed to the black & white Hoffman television on the counter by the sink.

"The God-damn Cubans," my father swore.

Mom, never swearing, but equally concerned, chimed in, "Bud, do you want some more coffee?"

Times were much different then. Fathers watched the news and dispensed infinite wisdom while mothers served coffee and made the kids cocoa! "But what about my photograph?" I asked.

In an ill-fated attempt to cure my teenage insecurity, I had sent a letter and photograph to Mary Hemingway in Ketchum, Idaho in 1960. I had asked her to have Ernest and Fidel Castro sign the photo. It was of their first meeting at the June 13, 1960 Hemingway International Marlin Tornea (Tournament) in Havana, Cuba. (Little did I know that 35 years later, I would be the sponsor of a boat of Americans in this same tournament.)

The look on my parents' faces as they watched the television was frightening. To see them frightened scared me. I went to my room confused— terrified and concerned about the difference in our routine home schedule. Television before dinner was never allowed.

Dinner was late that night, and the next day

the nuns had us all practice getting under our desks at school.

I never looked on a map for Cuba. It just seemed like a foreign place. Like Mars, with no real people, only aliens. In fact, my first impression of Cuba was much like watching the *Angry Red Planet* at the Kiggins theatre. We wouldn't see Mars, but we knew that they had plenty of 'invaders' to send to conquer earth! I was horrified by the confusion. I knew Mars was an enemy. The movies and comics of my youth told me so. But Cuba scared me even more because my parents told me it was real and they were scared, so I was scared. My fears of Cuba lessened with the arrival of new pimples and the 'Great October Wind Storm' in S.W. Washington, and to be quite honest, I did not think of the island again for some 30 years.

Incidentally, the signed photo returned to 4XXX S.W. Cherry St., Vancouver, WA, the day after President Kennedy announced a total embargo in Cuba in 1963. It has hung faithfully in my den ever since.

I first landed in Cuba sometime during 1990. Things were much different then. An American really had to be concerned about US Treasury prosecution for visiting this embargoed island and 'trading with the enemy'.

It is a story that, unto itself, would surely cause laughter and wonderment, but it was not my defining moment.

That moment came on the night of April 3, 1993.

"Cuba Libre!" And sometime after that remark, I uttered, "A father should never outlive his son."

Those words made up my very first real and meaningful conversation in Cuba. They were spoken in the lobby of the infamous Hotel Capri, soon after to be shut down for reasons of structural inadequacies rendering the building unsafe. Two 'likely to be arrested' aging gay men overheard my drink order, "Cuba Libre, por favor!"

They laughed.

I asked them to join me, and on that fateful April night my true Cuban adventures began— adventures which would set me on my course toward the dark horizon, laughing all the way to my inglorious end they tell me.

To tell you the story properly, though, I must first provide you with a little background on one of the most fascinating and influential leading characters during those early years.

Mariana's Story, or Mariana – a love story beneath the palms.

Mariana[2] was one of the local mysteries—a legend really.

---

[2] - Bob never provided her last name, if he even knew it.

Not even her many neighbors of Nautico, a once classy social center during the 1950s, about 15 minutes west from the area of Havana known as El Vedado and about 20 to 25 minutes from Central Havana and Old Havana, respectively, ever really knew where she came from or who she truly was. They couldn't even tell me how old she was. Some older neighbors said she had always lived there in the house. Others thought she had moved in a few years prior to the great revolution of 1958/59. The neighborhood kids were all certain she was an alien or a ghost, so it mattered little to them what the elders said.

As close to fact as there could be, I deduced the following: ET, as I called Mariana, back before the pre-ET movie times, had at least lived in the small room in the attic of the house I was now renting since the late 1940's. She had been a servant for the lady who owned the house and her crippled husband who rolled around in a wheel chair always yelling at Mariana because the antiquated wheel chair could never navigate the mop, broom, and cleaning rags she carelessly left behind on her daily duties.

I did discover an old black and white photo once of her standing next to a large house in some field which could have been anywhere on the planet. She looked to be in her teens. She had a ribbon in her hair and held the reins of a horse standing beside her, looking posed and very scared as she faced the photographer.

At the time I first rented the house and moved in, sometime during 1990, she was thought to be around 80 to108 years old. Truthfully, I could not tell the difference. I later (1993) uncovered the fact that she was 95, and was born the day the battleship *Maine*[3] was sunk. She never knew this fact, but she was aware that the revolution had taken place in 1959. She also knew who Fidel Castro, Che Guevara, and Camilo Cienfuegos Gorriarán were, although she had little interest in them or their cause.

Although we lived only one block from the ocean, she claimed she had not visited the seashore since 1947 (*more on this in a moment*).

We lived together for over three years, more blissful than husband and wife. She did not speak a word of English and I, no Spanish. After she died, I found a large knotty pine chest in her room filled with a wedding gown, my shirt and clothes, and many empty bottles of 5-year-old rum.

Apparently, once in the early pre-revolution 1950's, a Mexican doctor visited the previous owners of the house. During his stay, he reportedly proposed to Mariana. She apparently was so excited about such a prospect, she spent all her earnings on the bridal gown, veil, and chest.

He never came back.

Thus, the bridal souvenirs rested in the trunk

---

[3] - The battleship *Maine* sank on February 15, 1898.

gathering filtered dust until I discovered them two years after her death.[4] I do know a few personal things about her.

1. She loved to look at the bridal magazines I brought down for her from the USA each trip.
2. She was afraid of the beach which, as was stated earlier, was only one block from our house. One day, I took her in hand and tried to walk her to the seashore. After a few steps, when she knew where we were going, she sat down on the sidewalk and cried like a baby. No one knows why, but rumors were that once she went unauthorized and unescorted to the beach years ago, reportedly in 1947, as I said, and was severely reprimanded.[5]

Mariana Medico/Kitchen Habits

Three times a week, Mariana would depart the house early, often before anyone else was up, which did not necessarily mean early. On a few occasions, though, I was there to see her as she departed. She wore the same worn and tattered apron dress she always wore and left through the door with a colander under her arm. She would return late afternoon with the colander full of leaves, herbs, etc., and always some colorful flower stuck in her

---

[4] - Since Bob never gave the date of Mariana's death, we don't know when this occurred.
[5] - Who reprimanded her? Bob never said.

short nappy hair.

She never said a word to me coming in through the door, but went straight to the kitchen, cleared the counter top, opened the fridge, closed the fridge, opened a lower cupboard under the sink, pulled out an antique steel meat grinder just like Mom used to have. She performed this task in the absolute same order and with exacting precision. She would screw the meat grinder to the counter where a piece of linoleum had chipped away from years of use. Neither Mark or I ever figured out how those skinny, veined arms managed to turn the handle. Into it went the combination of leaves, grasses, herbs, and etc. Out came her green juice. Right into one of last night's empty rum bottles. We had to be very careful. If she could not find an empty, she would pour the rum out of one of ours.

She also always cleared away all our beer cans in the fridge to make room for her numerous and varied assortment of water bottles. I later learned from a neighbor that many years ago she fell in the kitchen and broke a hip. She could not move or get water for three days. I guess she never wanted to be without water again.

We never tasted the green concoction, but it must have been good for her.

****

A Boulder, Colorado friend of mine, Mark

(last name withheld) traveled to Cuba quite often with me, especially during 1993 through 1995. We stayed, on average, seven to ten days a month and then returned to Boulder for our jobs.

By this time, my 'in-country' partner, Jose Fuentes, was not only my friend, but my confidant, my facilitator, and my conscience. He was also my protector — mostly protecting me from myself. I'm sure that over the years I gave the poor man more nightmares about the *crazy gringo* running around his country making every mistake possible than he might care to remember, let alone confess to.

Anyway, on one particular amorous night sometime in 1993, Mark and I had earlier met two of Havana's most beautiful señoritas. One I nicknamed *the Madonna*, but her name was Anna. She was twenty and of Russian/Cuban decent. The other one was Beatrice. I called her *the beauty*. She was Cuban and nineteen years old. They were lovely jiniteras. We met them in a line of at least one hundred señoritas outside the gate to the moorings at the Marina Hemingway, which was located just outside of Havana. We drank rum, smoked cigars, and ate ham and cheese sandwiches at the Club Nautico cafeteria.

Later that evening, it began to rain hard. As the dancing is all done in the open air at Club Nautico, our dancing was brought to a soggy halt. We then decided to bring the girls back to my rented home in the Nautico residential area where Mariana and I lived.

As Marco and I approached her house under the crush of the deluge, we were slugging down rum. I suddenly realized that I had left my keys inside the house.

No problem, I thought as I attempted to rationalize my way through the dilemma. I figured my only hope was to knock on the door and Mariana, the ninety plus-year old black woman who lived in the attic of the rented house would come down from her room and let me in. She was the kindly sort. I knew that. I hated to disturb her sleep, but I had little choice.

Even though I had been to Havana several times before, I still felt the excitement of a new adventure as I knocked on the door of Calle 154. I knocked again and again only stopping long enough to take a swig from the bottle of Havana Club 7 Años that Marco and the giggling girls were passing between themselves.

The deluge continued unabated in cascading torrents, flooding the street with a literal river. We were all soaked to the skin, but no one minded at that point. We were operating on the promise of experiencing one of the real pleasures of Cuba in a private home in Havana, a rare and enjoyable diversion to the midnight bribes we had to pay to security at the Hotel Copacabana — a small incentive to the guards to allow us unmolested entry to our rooms with our ladies of the evening.

I banged on the door harder. No response. The door, blockaded with aluminum lawn chairs, an ingenious Cuban Burglar Alarm system, then took the brunt of my next assault well enough without surrender. No response. I was about to unload on it one more time when I stopped abruptly from shock. Stumbling back off the porch, caught completely off guard, I saw a pair of large, unblinking brown eyes staring back at me from behind the wood-louvered window beside the door. They finally blinked and then disappeared. We all heard a muffled cry of anguish – not fear – come from behind the door. Then the clatter of metal on marble, almost as irritating as the screech of a fingernail across a blackboard. She was repositioning the chairs inside—resetting the alarm system I presumed, while outside the drunken maniac American, drowning in the downpour, ran out of steam and ideas.

More noise and torrents of indistinguishable Spanish phrases then filtered out through the walls of the warm and dry home. We both turned to our new amigas pleadingly in hopes of understanding this new language and gaining entry to our home. After all, we had spent $100 that night even before treating our new dates to dinner and drinks.

So while families in Cuba huddled many to a room(s), we sought entry to a palatial private home by the sea. After a few minutes, the girls, including Mariana, hidden safely on the other side of the protective walls, were all talking. Mariana was gesturing in a 'go away' sign with a long wrinkled black arm waving between the slats of the window.

After a while though, 'Mariana' and 'mañana (tomorrow or in the morning)' were the only words I understood as the porch light went dark and the sounds faded. The girls both shrugged and our lack of Spanish and the girls' lack of English doomed us to another night of hotel bribery and cohabitation. In that instant, our well-planned promise of a private home of amour suddenly seemed like an all too typical ruse to the girls. They left right away as usual with their $20.00 in taxi money safely tucked in their purses along with the napkin-wrapped leftover slices of ever-present ham and cheese pizzas.

Mariana, I would discover later, forgot about us quickly and went back to her warm bed. She was not someone who tolerated fools, as we sadly learned.

It was no problem, my mind reasoned in continued and desperate rationalization, because Jose was my next-door neighbor. We would just go hang out at his house until we could figure how to get into mine. We knocked on the door. No response. Jose and his family were fast asleep, or ignoring us. Either way, it was raining and we had no place else to go locally.

We left the home, hailed a cab on 5th Avenue, a main thoroughfare leading back into the heart of

Havana, and went to the Cornodoro disco. Tomorrow we figured to get to the bottom of it. We would call David, the landlord, and explain our side of it. Later, we would approach the tenacious Mariana, trembling in our shoes, of course, and Calle 154 in daylight and without the girls.

After several more drinks, we hailed another cab and finally arrived at the ruinous Hotel, Neptino; we had just enough money left over to get a room and sleep it off.

The next day, after resupplying our cash, we arrived back at Mariana's house under the bombardment of rain once more. The front door was open. We hesitantly walked in. There was no sign of Mariana. I breathed easier. She scared me.

We cleaned up and walked over to Jose's house. He was resting in his chair as we walked in.

"We met two very lovely young ladies last night," I said.

"Oh yeah," answered Jose from his chair, matter-of-factly. It was no surprise to him.

"Yeah," I replied just as matter-of-factly.

"Where are they now?" he asked, only partially interested.

"Don't know."

That is how it was with Jose and me. We didn't need to say more than what was necessary. He was like a brother to me. I loved him like a brother.

Our once amorous evening now sadly behind

us, we felt betrayed. We felt swindled. Not by the young jiniteras, but by the dark and scary maiden of the house. Understanding our promised and expected sexcapade had been knowingly scuttled by an old woman, we decided to keep it a secret, being too embarrassed to admit it. Only Michael[6] would know of our failure, that is. Michael, the notorious, well-disciplined, and well-muscled first friend I met in Cuba over a year before.

Michael of Angola and Ethiopia. A picture of him with his troops in far away African lands that now graces my desk in a special place below that of his son in the uniform of Cuba's national baseball team. The very same Michael with whom I have shared my innermost secrets and, in return, only received a nod of understanding and another invitation to visit his family for lunch. A meal they struggled to afford on their own.

Cubans are that way with meals. No matter what hardships they are suffering, they, like Christ with the loaves and fishes, always managed to miraculously make the *pollo* and *fintas papas* last until everyone reclined in a near stupor of fullness — Michael, who shared with only me my first day in Havana.

Nautico Dart Club

On the morning of October 26, 1994, I started the *Nautico Dart Club* with fourteen neighborhood

---

[6] - Bob never disclosed Michael's last name.

kids. I set up a 6-foot-wide diameter plywood board with balloons on it (it was not easy to find the wood) and black t-shirts were provided to each kid.

Mariana, along with the neighborhood cats and dogs were none too pleased about it.

One observation about a country in need. Shirts were of dual purpose, first as uniforms and as real clothing. They had little option. To our great delight, we only lost two darts in one year. The kids were very insistent on finding any dart that went into the bushes by mistake.

Pina (Christmas 1997)

Steven, Stuart, and I (last names omitted for good reason) wanted to go to Cuba to see some friends for Christmas. We arrived to a pre-pope's visit (Feb 1998) and a very limited celebration atmosphere. Christmas has not been forbidden in Cuba, but was always very frowned upon by the government. In fact, a person was expected to show solidarity and go to work or school on Christmas Day. Absolutely no commercial promotions were allowed and the west's commercial excess (true) was mentioned as how Christmas was only a shopping holiday anyway.

We celebrated Christmas Eve in little Nautico Chapel with Jose's family and forty other local Cubans and pets. Mass was not present as I knew it. Only a play of Amal and the night visitor in the form of a valiant priest. Very different.

I bought everyone Cokes, hot dogs, and candy for a post *church* meal. The three of us were joined by Señor Pena (further identity was not provided) at the Nautico cafeteria for rum, cigars, and pizza. About twelve midnight, Pena stood up and started singing "mi three amigos from Colorado..." We were amazed by his beautiful voice. Apparently Pena used to be a teacher, but spent many years in a Cuban prison for subversive teaching. He was black and 70 years of age. He remained a good cigar-smoking amigo for a long time.

Pena was called 'radio man' by the neighborhood kids. He always listened to the short wave radio he made, and walked around the neighborhood reciting the news while he picked up trash and performed odd jobs.

Pig for a Party

After two weeks in the Nautico house, we were rapidly getting a very favorable reputation for hosting very large and fun Sunday fiestas. Thus, there was this one Sunday dilemma.

Jose was cooking in the walkway behind the house and sliding the cooked hamburgers through the wooden slats. We had already invited eighty-five people to our Sunday Blackjack party. Based on the failure of last week's Sunday fiesta, we felt we needed to be better prepared.

Last week's meal consumption for 85 hungry

and cash poor Cubans was: forty-five homemade pizzas, one hundred hamburger patties and homemade buns, 150 fried potatoes and servings of rice, 4 cases of Hatuey beer, 5 cases of Coca Cola and assorted sodas (7 Rapicola), and still we ran out. This does not count the ten bottles of five-year-old Havana Club rum.

What did we do to prevent this shortage? We sent our loyal but sex-induced driver Angel to find a pig the Saturday before the fiesta. He arrived promptly at 4:00 pm Saturday with a live squealing pig sitting, but tied down, in the back seat of his rusted Russian Lada Car.

"What the hell are we going to do with the pig?" we asked Angel.

"Cook it," he said.

"We don't know how!" we answered.

"OK," he said. He left us to join the pig in the car and drove off. No more words or advice were exchanged.

Promptly at 12:00 noon the following day (Sunday), Angel showed up and produced the pig splayed on a piece of plywood on top of his car. It covered most of the plywood board.

As we unloaded the cooked pig, I noticed that the plywood had a very faint balloon on it. It was the target board for my dart club the *Nautico Pirates*. I asked him why he used our club dart board. Angel only shrugged and said it was easier than finding another one!

If you understand about finding plywood in Cuba, it made all the sense in the world.

1994/1995 Vente Uno (21)

One of our neighbors had a great idea for the scorched plywood which formerly served as the table for our roasted pig, the remnant of our circular dart board.

"Cover it with green felt and let's make a Casino table," he suggested.

So we did!

We put it over the table in the living room, had Gloria (Jose's mother) sew some green felt on top and painted some meaningless white spots on top to simulate real poker chips. Thus, the *Saturday and Sunday Night Vente Uno (Blackjack)* games began. Six players at a time. Match sticks got boring very soon. Very soon, though, shots of rum, hamburgers, pizzas, and ham and cheese sandwiches, all became part of the 'pot.' We cleaned out our suitcases, shelves, fridge, to keep the pot filled with items the Cubans so badly needed.

Please remember that Mark (last name withheld) and I rented this wonderful house by the sea, but we didn't really live there. Only Mariana did. We never quite unpacked our suitcases, because as soon as we got home we would always start again to purchase all types of useful and needy items for the Cubans we loved — and the insatiable *Vente Uno* 'pot'.

Sometimes there were lines three deep behind each seated player, hoping for chance to play and win the pot for a hairdryer, bra, soap, shampoo, etc. Without Walgreen's weekly coupon specials in my local paper back home, the pot would have suffered greatly. We finally had to change playing rules so you had to get 21 twice in a row to win the pot. We couldn't keep up otherwise. I must also say that the players were from every walk of life and political party in Cuba.

Lobster Man and Son

During the spring of 1995, a black gentleman with his grandson would come by the house, with the child squashed into the basket of his dilapidated bicycle. I could smell him coming before I saw him. He always came when he knew I'd be home — around 5-6:00 p.m. — when I was sitting in my rocking chair on the porch. The lobster tail he was trying to sell me was always smelly and not fresh. I bought several a few times to only throw them away after he departed. $1.50 each for a 1.2 lb tail.

Jose had always warned me the lobster was bad (by the smell alone it wasn't hard to discern). In fact, Jose supplied me with my fresher seafood needs since he was an expert diver and fisherman.

"Just trying to help the old guy out," I explained to him.

"You're not really helping him," Jose said. "It only makes him think you're dumb and that old lobster is OK to sell."

Made sense.

Next trip, I bought a lot of school supplies for the boy. I gave them to the lad and had a chat with the old man about the bad lobster. He was very embarrassed, and after the bike rattled off that weekend, I never saw either of them again.

May 15-25, 2002

First two Eco Tour's went very well. I was able to sneak in twelve other *amigos* on the license. Val cancelled his wedding (he didn't really have a wedding to cancel, but I got him to leave his girl at home long enough to go with us). Interesting night to say the least. We had dinner at El Aljibe with Jimmy Carter. Well, to be honest, he wasn't there with *us*, but he was there with a huge entourage.

His speech later that evening made a very big impact on the average Cuban citizen who didn't know about the Varella Petition (11,000) signatures. Carter read his speech on National Cuban TV, in Spanish.

I didn't realize it at the time, but seating and attendance was heavily restricted because of security. To my absolute amazement, Sergio (owner of the restaurant) approved my entire group to be in attendance.

"Of course you'd be approved," said Val. "We're American and you're so very well known here. Sergio wouldn't dare turn you down."

He was right, of course, but it was still a shock to me.

Much later that evening, Val and I ended up on the patio of Hotel Nacional for what we used to call *sleep drinks*. We saw Jimmy Carter walk through the lobby. He didn't notice us at all. We sat chatting out on the patio about how successful the trip had been so far. We both believed then that Eco Tours would be solidly in our future. It was good to just sit and chat without entertaining clients. With Val, I could always just be myself. It can get pretty stressful at times. I was having a great evening until Val's 'wife' showed up and dragged him home. (For the record, Val was not really married, but she owned him. I think he was whipped, but he'll never admit it.)

My End is Nigh, but I Fail to Cry

I heard the harsh, threatening voice as the gun poked into my back. "Give me your fuckin' wallet!" he yelled.

"Go fuck yourself!" I yelled, actually backing against the barrel of the gun in my lower back.

After all, it was only last night that I'd failed in a bungled suicide attempt. "You're a blessing in disguise," I whispered to the unknown assailant. "I beg you to kill me! I want to die!"

Somehow I secretly hoped it would end this way. Someone else would have the courage to take the life I so much hated after a lifetime of failures.

But I did not think it would happen in the streets of Havana, a city I had grown to love, a country which seemed to welcome me for what I was, not what I feared I wasn't or what I hadn't accomplished in my 48 years. Where had my Havana gone? I thought as the stranger's hand reached for my wallet. It now seemed like every nigger in Cuba had a gun. And, every jinitera[7] had a price tag of a new suit hanging off them.

It all seemed to change when the two planes were shot down and Fidel had to move to Spain. At least we thought he was in Spain. *The Virgin(s) of Holava*!

Fidel and the Magic Act, a passing thought

All of Cuba is the curtain behind which the magician hides. Just like the 'Wizard of Oz' in a previous land, he maintains his silent presence. The sugar cane continues to grow; the demand for his cigars increases daily and US Presidents continue to fall by the wayside.

Still, the Cuban 'ship of state' proceeds on course, bow slicing through the wind, as seasonal, natural, and political maelstroms continue to besiege this once 'island Paradise.' On the bridge, far above the bow wave's mist, the ship's captain continues on unmolested. The ship cuts through the sea of despair

---

[7] - Jineteras are often confused with common prostitutes. This is not true. The literal translation of the word is "jockey" but the word jinitera goes much deeper than that. Jiniteras are born out of the economic woes of Cuba and are unique to Cuba in that regard.

as if on automatic pilot. With land all around, but no port of refuge in sight, the bilge pumps ineffective and sorely in need of immediate repair, the ship suddenly takes on water. But El Maximo Capitan continues onward, with discarded food stuffs and much needed supplies floating in its wake. Temporarily lighter, the ship of state continues onward. Eagerly confronting the next inevitable disaster in its path. Problems are temporarily solved, with only a few million more people hungry for the discarded and much needed supplies rapidly sinking in the ship's devastating churn of the sea.

Cuba Interrupted
VIRGO (Aug 23-Sept 22): (Robert's Horoscope 2009) - *Invitation to travel could be accompanied by substantial check. Surprises due, long-distance communication relates to publishing advertising, fashion news. Sagittarian is in picture.* (Robert's birthday is September 2nd.)

After eleven years of successful tours to Cuba, I now found myself encamped in the East Cape of South Africa with four amigos. We originally set out 6/19/02 for two weeks of bird hunting in Cape Town, SA. Sounded logical, right? Why not? Take some of your best adventure-seeking Cuba veterans and give them a new sponsored experience. Looked great on paper. Looked great in the color brochures they sent me. Hell, it just looked great!

Let me tell you.

Departed Denver for Atlanta 12:00 6/19. No problems.

Then, the proverbial 'shit hit the fan.' My pre-assigned seat on the aisle was rejected. What? That's when the 15½ hour, *middle seat in couch* nightmare began!

Video box was under the seat in front. Leg room minimal. Complaints? None yet! It must have been a mistake. Surely it will end right. Well, it did not. Six movies later, we landed in Cape Town, SA.

Groggy, sore, tired, confused, and darkness at 8:00 a.m. (possible?) Yes. We were south of the equator; after all, 6/21/02 was the solstice. Bathroom, taxi, hotel. Breakfast we never remembered....

On 6/22, not nearly rested enough, but somewhat oriented, we left Cape Town for Port Elizabeth, launch point for my first Africa shooting safari. To Woolworths for clothing, bottle shop for booze, and did I forget to mention, the Rand to dollar exchange?

(1) Bottle vodka
(1) Bottle gin
(1) Bottle champagne
(1) Bottle scotch
(1) Bottle brandy
(12) Small tonics

How much? $44.00. I am now moving my

addiction to South Africa.

So far, so good! Departed in a convoy for the mountain region NE of Port Elizabeth supposedly a two-and-a-half-hour trip. After four hours, we asked the guide, Arnold, how much farther?

"Ten minutes," he replied.

One hour and 60 KM later, we finally turned off the gritted dirt road to where we were to stay. As I write this, I can't tell you where we are. Really. Africa? Yes, I know that because I flew somewhere 15½ hours SE across the Atlantic.

But, as we all continually remarked, "it looks just like Colorado," from where we just came. How is this possible? Don't get me wrong. The lodge is great. The hospitality, welcomed and wonderful, but we can't be in Africa.

"Fine," our hosts said, "but the bird hunting is the best in the world."

"OK," I agreed.

We enjoyed dinner and then drinks over political discussions.

"Africa?" I inquired, as the snow began to fall.

"Yes," was the response.

"Really?"

I am sitting here in the main dining room of the lodge drinking brandy at 11:00 a.m. writing these notes as the hail, snow, and rain falls on the roof. Bird hunting tomorrow?

I came to South Africa with my 'special'

group to do a video segment on South Africa bird hunting. I intended to use it on my website. However, here I am still writing while the others are in bed wearing long johns, huddled under electric blankets, sleeping, and awaiting the dawn of their first South Africa bird hunt.

I go outside to reassure myself that I am indeed in South Africa. Yes, I see a palm tree in the moonlight. No, I do not see snow. But, how in the hell am I going to tell everyone back home that we are hunting in long johns in South Africa?

6/23 — First day of the hunt — the night before. I missed one thing. Politics! We sat around the fire with cigars, brandy, male and female and tried to figure out world politics. Great experience but just impossible. I went to sleep that night greatly depressed. Not unhappy, but confused! Why? Because the world problems can never be solved! By the way, who are we on this unusual safari?

1. Bob Woly - Havana Host
2. Joe 'The Shark' Brino, guest
3. Michael 'The 82nd' Carmichael, guest
4. Don 'Hollywood' Bofer, guest
5. Chris 'the Kid' Bourbon, guide
6. Arnold, 'The Mummy' Slablent
7. AC – host – hunting guide
8. Minnie – cook and diplomat
9. Benton – black teacher who slept in a shack

Africa, who needs it? Who really gives a shit? Glad HIV is in Africa? Maybe all are true. But guess what? We all came from Africa and most likely, most of us will die in Africa. Probably of HIV, the equalizer. It's a shame for two reasons: One, it needlessly and unfairly selects its victims, and two, Africa and its darkness was every boy's dream.

At least it was my dream.

An Alcoholic's Search for the Elusive Taliban Falconry Camps, or, Traveling like an American

---

I killed a man in a fight July 2, 1980, in a bar called *Franco's Hidden Harbor,* exactly nineteen years after Ernest Hemingway took his own life with the shotgun previously used by his father to take *his* own life. I never believed this until I went to Afghanistan.

Suicide by Taliban

That's what Val called it. Before I left, he said he understood why I was going to Afghanistan. "You want to commit *suicide by Taliban*, if you can," he boldly stated.

"No," I argued, "I want to go to study falconry."

"Bullshit! You're lying to yourself, Bob," the bastard insisted. "You want go out in a blaze of glory and be mentioned on the nightly news; that's what you want."

Damn Val, anyway. He had a way of seeing right through me, and I think he enjoyed calling me out.

"It would be exciting," I finally admitted.

"Well. I think you're nuts," he retorted. "But it's your life, buddy. You have a right to do as you like. I hope, though, that when you get over there and see just what's going on, you'll discover the real truth of it and find out you want to live. So, I'll just say to you, I hope you go there, rediscover your purpose, and come back home safe and sound."

Damn Val! Damn him! Why did he have to say it that way? Now what the fuck am I going to do? How can I go out in glory knowing that someone knows my secret?

Was this trip possibly my own attempt at suicide, as Val had suggested? If so, did traveling to Afghanistan make it seem more explainable with higher, more socially acceptable overtones? At least that is what my addiction counselor at the VA informed me the day prior to my departure from the USA.

As I departed, I hoped both he and Val were wrong and I was right.

****

To digress a bit, something awoke me during the night before I was to leave. Not a dream or nightmare, but something more sinister. I awakened sweating and frightened, but I still felt her beside me, a really faithful lady, my 12 gauge Mossberg shot gun with an illegal sawed-off barrel and a pistol grip.

However, in getting up, I realized her sister was no longer beside me. She lay sprawled on the floor beneath my feet, the many Oxycodone tablets that had spilled from an illicit prescription bottle.

And the third sister, known as *Lady Luck*, was preening in the gray hours before dawn as she always did on such an occasion. Nothing seemed to bother her. She only cared about 'she.'

Shit!, I thought. Once again a bottle of booze was not enough to give me the courage to do it. I guess I'll have to go to Afghanistan after all.

****

Before I continue, let me tell you a story of my first experience with suicide. I can safely tell the story now for the first time because Mom, Dad and dear sister Jo are deceased, and I no longer consider the person of whom I'm speaking to be a family member.

It was a rainy school night in Vancouver, Washington when I heard the click of a round being chambered in a shot gun. I knew the sound very well from the many times I had gone duck and pheasant hunting with Mom and Dad.

I looked back into 'our' bedroom. I saw him sitting on the bed with a shot gun in his mouth and a pillow cushioning the stock imbedded in his lap. I knew what was up.

I knew exactly what he felt. My brother that is — but I'd never discussed it with anyone. How could I at age 13? And, because of that, it really didn't frighten me to see my brother that way.

Nothing new really! Just something that would certainly get the parents excited and concerned. I will remember this ploy for later.

I ran down the stairs and awakened Mom and Dad. Only Dad responded. I guess mothers were not supposed to handle such problems. They made lunches, smiled, and just loved us as kids.

Dad pushed me aside and ran up the stairs to our bedroom. He slowly opened the door and told me to stay in the hall. "Don't come into the bedroom," he whispered.

A whispered command from my father really didn't scare me all that much, so I went into the adjoining bathroom, opened the medicine cabinet, grabbed a glass, and put it to the inner wall. I had seen this on Mission Impossible. And, it worked.

I heard everything. Surprisingly, I cried but did not put the glass down.

I heard them both speak. And, for the first time in my life, I realized I loved my brother. We were the same in our loneliness and unhappiness. Unfortunately for him, I was the better athlete.

He didn't shoot himself that wintry night, but simply disappeared. It was some months before I even got a chance to talk to him. I knew from that moment on that suicide was a sweet revenge on parents and yourself. I loved the concept, but was too small to hold a shotgun in my mouth.

Decades later, I once again encountered

suicide. However, this time it was much more personal, and I had gained some valuable 'first hand' experience in the matter. I had actually tried it, on many occasions.

It was a very cold and dry winter evening in Boulder, Colorado. The Boulder Community Hospital staff was used to cold weather, as was I and the 'street persons' who were driven inside the ER seeking heat and/or medical assistance.

I had a late night shift as a volunteer and was bored chasing the homeless back out into the streets of a privileged town that denied their very existence.

Then, the sliding doors opened and a gust of snow and freezing wind jarred me from my half sleep as the two of them came into the ER.

I immediately recognized them as students. After all, Boulder was a college town! I could smell their drunkenness (Jägermeister shots I guessed), and caught the badges on their left arms that I readily recognized as homemade tourniquets…on their pale and adolescent wrists.

They didn't smile. They didn't do anything but shiver and hug each other as they approached the ER administration desk where I worked.

That was when the ER doctor approached them with an equally reproachful attitude. He simply said, "Follow me." No please or other consideration.

I followed as I was not supposed to do, and went into the ER room. When I heard what the doctor said, I went crazy. Or ballistic. Whatever. I let him know what I thought and lost my volunteer job as a result. But I gained two friends in the process with whom I still speak some twenty years later.

In short, what transpired between the ER doctor and the two kids was this:

"What happened?" the doctor asked one of the kids.

"We tried to commit suicide," was the answer.

Then the doctor said, "I know how you feel!"

That's when I entered the room and shoved the doctor against the wall, shouting at him, "Bullshit! Have you ever tried to commit suicide? I have, and I know how they feel, not you!"

It turns out that the kids' parents had allowed them to come to CU together if they both got straight A's. They didn't, and they didn't want to be separated from the bonds of adolescent love. Puppy love, we cynical lot who do not remember, call it.

I know this is supposed to be a travel journal, but I must get this suicide issue off my mind before we actually start the journey. After all, it is truthfully why I was going to Afghanistan in the first place.

Damn Val! Damn him!

As a special note, I will admit, concerning my suicide attempts, I never once called 911. And, of course, each and every attempt failed. But each attempt occurred with a humbled discretion and in the comfort and privacy of my own home.

But, I did learn from my brother and myself that to be successful at suicide one needed to have courage, courage enough to commit a cowardly act. In fact, suicide and its failed attempts brought out the cowardice in me for the first time.

Shakespeare? Are you listening?

Two weeks later I was packed with every survival item that REI had to offer. How ironic really? Survival gear? Well, I guess I had to stay alive until I was able to kill myself. Or, be killed.

It kind of made sense at the time. After all, everyone loves a survival story.

Oh, by the way, I was also onto a very unknown story about the Taliban falconry camps in Pashtun Province, Afghanistan.

But, to hell with the story and its research, it was just a wonderful and heroic 'cover' for a suicide!

Booze on the Run! or, An Alcoholic's Escape into Afghanistan!

Where to start? Too much happening too fast!

"One-way Business Class to New Delhi," I asked Glennis, my faithful travel agent of twenty years. "The cost doesn't matter. And, as soon as possible."

"But, one way is so much more expensive," she responded. "And, you need to come back!" I hung up, realizing I was not really going to India, but going to Afghanistan. I had previously applied for, and received, multiple entry visas to India, Pakistan, and Afghanistan for just such an occasion.

Why multiple entry visas? Well, just maybe I might have to use them.

I then went online to Travelocity and purchased a one-way return trip ticket from New Delhi to Portland, Oregon. No one would know, it being the private act of a coward who did not have the courage to kill himself already. I knew the cost was not an issue because once dead, money would not matter.

But it surely would to someone who inherited it! The debt that is.

And, I wondered how many 'Sky Miles' would I accrue from Delta for my one way trip to heaven or hell?

****

On September 2, 2009, my birthday, I departed Chicago via Frankfurt to Chicago. Business class was luxurious. Late on my birthday night I met Monika who boarded in Frankfurt. We spent eight wonderfully romantic hours just talking. Also met India's Foreign and Finance Ministers.

Many hours later, I found myself lying on the cold concrete floor of the New Delhi Airport, awaiting a Kam Airlines flight to Kabul, Afghanistan — via the 'back door' as they say —

longing for a beer while listening to the prayer chants of the only other six passengers waiting to board our flight.

Ironically, and with some prejudice, I noted that the only place they had to spread their prayer rugs was in the entranceway of a not yet opened terminal bar. The neon beer signs created a surrealistic shadow on the prayer rugs as the penitents bowed in holy submission to someone far away who could not make the airplane take off on time.

When the airport loudspeaker announced the departure of our flight, 'they' gathered their prayer rugs and lined up at the check-in counter the same as I. *Why was one DC3 airplane taking only us seven to Kabul?* I suspiciously wondered. And, via the 'back door' I might add?

Moments later, we all boarded the shuttle taking us from the airport to the plane. That is when two of the Muslims arose as one and sent a chill up my spine. They grabbed my arms and seemed to relieve me of my briefcase. Then gently lifting me up onto the boarding platform, they escorted me to my seat, placing my briefcase on my lap.

One said, in Oxford English, "Sir, we noticed you had trouble walking and had a limp. Are you okay?"

I clutched my briefcase, which held my funds, and responded, "Thank you. And, yes, I am okay!"

Little did they know that during this holy

month of Ramadan, one year before, I had injured myself with an alcoholic 'breakdown' in Banff, Canada while attending my nephew's wedding.

But none of this really explained how the Taliban earned over $20 million a year legally selling rare falcon chicks to the kings, princes, and sheiks of the United Arab Emirates. This is what I precisely wanted to find out, and the only way to do that was to blindly travel to the Pashtun Province in Afghanistan and see for myself.

I boarded the plane, a DC 3 prop: I knew this plane well; it was on my logo for my company, *Last Frontier Expeditions*. I'd also flown on one during my past travels to Africa. We seven had much room to spare, but still we sat apart. The six of them and I. The flight was to be short I had been told. Just over Pakistan and to Afghanistan. I checked my passport(s) and decided the Irish one would be best. I already had my visa, so clearing customs and immigration should be quite simple. But, as the wheels touched down, I did not yet know that I'd landed at the wrong airport according to my understanding.

****

My Arrival

I entered Afghanistan via the 'back door' as I previously mentioned with the, as also aforementioned, fabricated intent of conducting research for a book I was planning to write entitled, *On the Front Lines of Recovery: An alcoholic's search for the elusive Taliban falconry camps.* I did indeed visit one such camp and am having a book printed about the journey.[8]

I arrived in Kabul, Afghanistan late at night via a Kam Airlines vintage DC-3 airplane. I landed at the little-used Kabul International Airport, as I soon found out. Almost all international airlines land at Kabul's nearby Bagram Air Force Base controlled by the US military.

Of possible interest? Kabul was chosen Afghanistan's capital in the year 1776!

I cleared customs, and then walked about a block to 'I knew not where.' There were no taxis or cars and the few other passengers had simply disappeared into the darkness of the city. I stood on a curb and waved at an approaching pair of headlights. I suppose 'pair' is an overstatement!

A, what else, Toyota pickup truck, *technicals,* as they call them, pulled to the curb with three uniformed police, or soldiers for that matter, inside who waved me over as they came to a halt under one of the only working street lights.

No words were yet spoken as they generously ushered me inside to the passenger seat after instructing one soldier to exit the seat and sit in the back of the truck with the machine-gun-toting

---

[8] - The book was never completed, but morphed into his exploits in Afghanistan.

guard.

"Where are you going? And who are you?" the driver uttered in pretty good English.

"I am going to the Canadian Embassy," I replied, "and I am an Irish citizen visiting Afghanistan for research on my book about falconry." (Almost a true story except for the Irish bit and the book, I guess.)

The drive was mostly bumpy and very silent as we drove through the seemingly deserted streets. I gazed in awe at a city I never knew really existed except in the news. I just thought it was a war zone.

We safely passed a high-rise shopping center, four- and five-star hotels, and a citizenry walking the *pre-curfew* infamous 'Chicken Street', seemingly unafraid and conducting business in a *pre-curfew* frenzy. I was told that this market street was the only one that openly operated at this time of night. That explained the dark and deserted streets I'd seen as I came from the airport.

Arriving at the Canadian Consulate, I jumped out of the truck, grabbed my pack from the rear, and stood completely confused as to what I should pay for this unsolicited generosity. "$20 dollars a person," I was told. "No problems, and when dark, it is most dangerous," the voice added. $20 dollars each it gladly was! The truck left and disappeared around the next corner without waves exchanged just as the guard in the bunker at the entrance to the Canadian Consulate motioned me over to him.

"Come in where it's safe," he told me. I did and sat on a pile of sand bags cradling my pack and fingering my money belt for the umpteenth time since I'd entered the Toyota pickup at the airport. Both were safe and sound.

"Wait a minute," he added as he picked up a phone and muttered something to someone apparently inside the consulate.

In what seem instantaneous, two burly soldiers appeared. One grabbed my pack and the other helped me up to a standing position. With little fanfare, we entered the dimly lit night and walked across the now deserted 'Chicken Street' to I knew not where.

There was very little conversation as we maneuvered around broken cement sidewalks and downed tree limbs before entering a dark alley a block and a half from the consulate.

"There is where we are going," one said, pointing to a dim light half a block in the distance. "That is the 'Palace' compound for foreigners." In what seemed like only a step or two, we three were standing behind yet another well-armed sand-bagged bunker.

"He needs a room. I do not know for how long," one said. The Afghani guard nodded and motioned me to enter the bunker. I never saw the Canadians depart. Nor did I see them again. Most likely I would not remember what they looked like anyway.

That night I was much too disoriented and frightened to remember much of anything.

Into the bunker I went like Alice through the proverbial looking glass. Then into another bunker and through a metal door that was raised with much noise but much less fanfare. Wow! I thought as I stood before what looked like a real hotel reception area. I hurried in and approached the desk to met a person who did not yet know that he was soon to be my first and best Afghan 'best friend."

I slept very uneasy through what was left of the night. Not yet unpacked and not even bothering to find a tooth brush and tooth paste to brush my teeth. No, I was too tired, drained from fear and exhaustion, so I just lay down on my small bed, face first, clutching a pillow, and went to sleep.

The Language of the Burqa

I have no idea what time it was the next morning when I heard numerous tappings on the glass and rolled over to witness some 'backlit' apparition standing in my window. This was to be my first encounter with the infamous 'Blue Burqa.' It seemed both curious and frightening as the tapping continued.

I got out of bed wearing last night's sweat-smelling and wrinkled clothes and walked to the door. Opening it, I found myself face to face with what seemed like a blue Halloween costume. She (it) softly pushed me aside and set her cleaning bundle on my bed. As if to say, "you are not going back to sleep. It is time to get up!"

In fact, as if she was not sure I got the message, she pushed the blue sleeves of her burqa up to her elbows as if ready to get to work.

I nodded, left $5 on the television, and walked down to the sunlit courtyard. I had not even noticed it the night before. Now it was occupied by the most interesting and diverse group of people I had ever seen.

People working on computers, others reading, some just sunbathing, and small groups talking. But, almost all, I noticed, were smoking — even the old Afghani man in the corner trying to sell carpets and scarves to a crowd that was not interested in the least.

After a couple of nods and hellos, I was directed to a small breakfast room. Breakfast was not bad, but not warm either. Oh well, nothing ventured, nothing gained, I thought as I approached the front desk manned by a young man with an even younger boy. He spoke excellent English. The boy was his brother. In about a half-hour he explained almost everything I thought I needed to know about my stay.

He arranged for a driver, translator, and guard to meet me in the courtyard early the next morning. The burqas? They were all women (of course) who did the cleaning and laundry for the guests.

"They are usually the wives of the guards, so

be very careful how you communicate with them," the small boy warned me.

Back in my room, I found the 'burqa' gone and the room clean. The five-dollar bill was still there. This does not happen elsewhere, I thought. The next morning I was up very early and sat in the courtyard until breakfast when I witnessed a sea of burqas approaching. Maybe ten in all. They all looked the same… except for different colored, imitation, plastic 'Crocs' on their feet … a wave of larger than life, blue-colored, Casper the Ghosts!

That is the moment I devised my plan. It was actually an Afghan epiphany, in fact: *Always remember my 'burqa's' shoe color.* I remembered mine was lavender in color. Should be quite easy as I didn't think they readily traded shoes. But, I remembered, they always removed their shoes before entering a household. I would have to be very careful and find one other substantiating characteristic about my burqa.

Throughout the ensuing days of my stay, I was able to communicate with my 'burqa' in a fashion that always started with recognizing her shoes. She would always bow when entering the room, and soon she began taking my tips and actually became comfortable enough to ask if she could borrow a magazine or two. Sure, I thought. Anything to undermine this fundamentalist Islamic society and help our war effort in the process, I hastily concurred.

But the 'burqa' and I became friends. We nodded and chatted. Anyone who knows me knows that I did most of the talking! We never touched. But, on special occasions, she adjusted her burqa so that I could see her face, if only faintly, behind the viewing screen of her head piece. This was quite an honor, and I knew it.

Sometime later that week, I told some of the others in the courtyard, non-Americans, about my 'burqa'. They only laughed and said, "You Americans." Then went back to conversing among themselves about 'we Americans' as if I was not even there.

September 12, 2009 - Kabul

I found myself sitting in a hotel courtyard in Kabul vomiting continually and violently for no apparent reason. I considered the reason to be either anxiety or lack of sleep, or perhaps both. Nights in bed were horrible. Dreams were continuous and nightmarish. Even sleeping during the day brought mind-boggling nightmares. Always last! Even bad dreams when I'm with Monika. But those dreams were always drawn forth from a lack of self-confidence. In emotional turmoil? Yes! Very! But always with an unsettling undercurrent of fear as their basis. Even a cigar did not settle me down. I took six Tylenol PMs at that very moment and tried to sleep. Helicopters screamed overhead from every direction, all day and night!!

Sirens, sirens, sirens. They do not frighten me. Yet they serve to remind me of the too numerous crimes I have committed, and the remembrance of having escaped from the punishment due me! As the sirens fade into the distance, I welcome their retreat.

I saw a small hawk on the roof of the hotel today. He seems to be as misguided as I. He was surely in the wrong place for hunting. Maybe I was also in the wrong place? When I looked again, it was gone. For some selfish and cruel reason, its disorientation made me happy for the first time in a while. I wonder if it felt the same about me. But then, hawks were not human, so they did not think such cruel thoughts!

Heard from my driver regarding Ramadan: "the bigger the mosque, the more words you can say in it."

And, maybe it would be okay, just for today, if I went into the local Afghan fried chicken franchise and got us some chicken and cokes? Whomever was on the sign sure looked like colonel Sanders in a turban!

I saw my beloved hawk this morning just after sunrise. At least I will pretend it is the same hawk. 'IT' is now a 'he.' Just as I hope he does not consider me the sorrowful 'he,' that he pondered yesterday.

He made a screeching hawk sound and ascended towards the cobalt blue Kabul sky. But not before he dropped a feather into the rose bushes below. As I bent to retrieve his gift, I accidentally smelled the roses!

I can no longer record my musings by days. The thoughts come much too sporadically, and the Afghans surely do not think in 'days'! History has taught them to think in decades and centuries. We, as a nation, are not old enough to have such thoughts. As the war in Afghanistan clearly demonstrates, we are only capable of an optimistic foresight. Not a realistic hindsight.

Such is war as practiced by the West!

Traffic in Afghanistan is truly a 'full contact' sport. I was reminded of this today as I watched USC defeat OSU in football. Funny how it took a trip across the world to even care about such a game?

And, unlike the contact sports I've played, the color of the uniform or the make of the mascot does not really matter along the congested, unmarked, pot-holed streets of Kabul.

A new and costly Mercedes Benz has no advantage over a rusted Datsun pickup truck or a family-filled Corolla. It is nose-to-nose and always a head-to-head confrontation. Up the middle and always 'over center!'

I am overhearing a conversation now. "How many trucks are missing? Where are the materials?"

The helicopters are quiet today. It's Sunday. We take a break from the war on Sundays. They never take a vacation from war. They have not done so in hundreds of years — maybe thousands. But their commerce does close on Fridays whereas in the West, ours never does. Gone is the Sabbath and the 'Blue Laws' of the West, and my youth.

I went blindly into the depths of Kabul for lunch today. Arrived eventually 45 minutes later at a heavily fortified Chinese restaurant — the 'Golden Pagoda' it was called — I entered alone and ate, alone!

While perusing the menu, I had a typically American thought, "It sure seemed expensive for an advertised budget restaurant in Kabul — or for that matter, anywhere. And, with the cost of the taxi, it was downright expensive! Then, when the food arrived, I realized that the cost was only expensive in the calories and over-abundance of food I had ordered. Been there, done that, many times before!

Thought about having a beer with lunch. Did not. Not because I didn't want to secretly imbibe, but rather because of the $12 cost. I'm sure my substance abuse counselors back home would not consider this reluctance a positive step in my continued treatment. More of a temporary but abhorrent form of aversion therapy. As I sit here in the courtyard writing and smoking a cigar, I realize the double, 20 ft high hotel security gates also do not take Sunday off. They continue to slam with the false sense of security they provide.

Although my lunch had not yet begun to

settle, I did not vomit it up. Progress 'one step at a time,' as they say. As I casually watch the sun set, I will take progress in any 'way, shape, or form!'

Night time does not descend in Kabul. It arrives suddenly as the security doors cease to slam closed or cease to creak open. Their work is hopefully done for another day. We are inside and the enemy is outside!

Monika was right. The Afghani men's casual wear was indeed very handsome. It sure feels good not to be depressed, or to worry. But, as to being happy? I am not equally as sure. It is still very new to me and possibly not deserving! We'll see! I am, however, slowly becoming more receptive to happiness just as I am about not wanting to be depressed. Tonight I will leave Paul Bowles alone under the sheltering sky where he belongs. I still do not know why I am here in this god-forsaken place, but I do know I love it here more every minute. I only hope I am not seeking something at their warm and welcoming expense.

Earlier today I asked a man why the trees around the hotel compound were missing so many limbs. He shrugged his shoulders, pointed, and responded, "last year a Taliban fired a RPG from the tree into the hotel courtyard. Killed seven foreigners!"

Too bad for their families, I thought. *But they should not have been here in the first place* — then I thought about the very grass upon which I had just thoughtlessly snuffed out my cigar. *I feel more sorrow for the trees and grass and flowers destroyed by the blast! I'll keep that thought to myself at least until I return safely home!*

Saw my first kites today — flying high overhead and dipping perilously in and out of the sunset. Wish I could have seen the boys flying them, but they were safely outside the security gates. Surely doing something they had done so many times before: flying because the weather was still optimum and the winds benevolent. Like all of life in Afghanistan, they didn't know what tomorrow would bring — maybe a fair dawn? Or, possibly the torrential rains that would accompany tomorrow's monsoon? The kites flew into the darkness as if there might not be a tomorrow. Too bad the foreigners killed in the courtyard did not possess such wisdom?

I must stop writing now. I am exhausted of thought and finally, pleasantly tired!

The dawn did not beckon me as I had hoped. The sky was more than impending with storm. The hawk was not there to greet me. No feathers in the rose garden. Had 'my hawk' (My hawk? No more mine than the polar bears in the zoo of my youth.) failed me? Did he no longer have patience for my sorrows? There were also no kites in the sky. Only the severed and charcoal limbs of the trees the Taliban had so recently favored.

As my thoughts of self-destruction returned, I

headed for the very place I shouldn't – now I know why I enjoy watching track and field so much. Yes, it is the superbly conditioned physiques. But, more important (at least to me) is that they are not afraid to clap at the crowd before they have even completed an event. If only the overpaid, over-glamorized, diuretic, and anorexic runway models would realize the true beauty of a Croatian woman high jumper's ass!

But then, I do not think the high jumper finds the absence of the runway model's ass a thing of beauty either.

Does the long jumper whose 'six pack' clearly shows through his Nike t-shirt really need to work out anymore?

Maybe what I truly enjoy about the track athlete's body is what I detest about my own body!

I awakened later that night with a smile. No, not because I had dreamed of sex with the Croatian high jumper with the equally beautiful ass, but because I found my hand nestled comfortably down the front of my underwear and I felt truly alive like I had not felt for such a very long time.

But then, things quickly returned to normal as I rolled over onto the remote TV control and thought it was a big piece of beef jerky!

The pathetic rcfrain I heard coming from Room 121 over and over one evening. Helen! Helen! Please listen to me. My job is over in two weeks. Are you coming with me? Helen! Helen! I told you I am leaving and not coming back to Kabul again! Helen! Helen! The final plea is perfect oxford English. Then, shit! And the phone slams into the Bakelite cradle and the door slams shut! *Been there. Done that!* I thought sorrowfully.

Tonight was the first night I didn't see or hear the choppers flying overhead. Even the dove under the eave above my door was silent. Then I heard it for the first time in my life! The wonderful musical song of the call to prayer from a local Muadhin. Enchanting. Then, just as suddenly as it had begun, it ended. The sound of a woodpecker nearby joined me and then the memory of the frightening and all too familiar sounds of the Chinooks which had awakened me that morning resurfaced.

I am oh so glad I didn't write down my hasty and bigoted thoughts of a few hours prior. Because if I'd done so, I would now be shamefully tearing out the pages of my wonderful leather-bound journal and tearing them up in remorse.

Maybe later, when I've finished my travel missive, if I feel they are important to my story, I will include them as an addendum? But now, back to the wonder period a few hours hence!

I was watching a group of Africans this evening in the courtyard as they were watching the shadows of darkness approach. Together they nodded in unison. I learned later that they were awaiting a group decision as to when Ramadan had ended for that day. Then their dinner was served at a communal table. Before they started to eat, I approached them with an apology for possibly interrupting their ritual.

Of course, I did not want to intrude upon their repast. I only wanted to know if the smoke from my cigar (although across the courtyard) would be offensive to them. Once again (in unison) they said, "No! Surely Not!" I returned to my own table and put out my cigar anyway. In the scheme of things, my evening ritual just did not seem as important as their evening ritual!

I thought of the smoking issue as the result of what I'd heard today! Apparently an American soldier (why does it always seem to be an American) got into a fight over the issue of drinking water and smoking during Ramadan. The fight escalated. They shot each other dead as well as an innocent bystander who was way too young to even consider smoking. A shame? Or, just another day in life on the streets?

Slept quite well last night. At least I do not remember any bad dream. Lo and behold, the Tylenol PMs were still sitting on the glass shelf above the sink in the morning. Wouldn't my VA shrink be proud of me! Must have been the mind-numbing 167 to 123 cricket match on the 'Telly.' Australia won. Sri Lanka lost. Who really gives a shit as long as it induced sleep?

If another match does so again, then off to the Kabul patent office to register such as a very effective anti-insomnia remedy. I have not been so mentally exhausted since my first game of Donkey Pong on my 20 lb Atari so many eons ago. Off to Lake Qargha for some fishing. No one seems to know if there are any fish in the lake, but who cares. I don't! Patrick Swayze died today as did, I am sure, a soldier somewhere in this country.

Suffering greatly from my alcohol induced neuropathy — feet so numb and cold that it affects my ability to walk (hobble really) greatly. Must have broken a toe or two last night. Toes swollen and bruised more than usual. Gave away my new and expensive REI hiking boots some days ago. They hurt my feet too much. I now wear Afghani slippers or my gym shoes with the toes cut out. Quite a fashion statement for the locals. Just can't seem to jar my memory enough to discuss the daily flights of the Chinooks, and writing this 'whatever' is also becoming a real chore. In fact, a real 'pain in the ass!' I fear forgetting them has actually taken some joy out of my trip. Maybe I will take a break today and just let my camera and mouth do the talking? Maybe not?

Fishing beckons much too early on a morning without hot water!

12:00 Back from lake trip. All my dreams are fulfilled! Might as well board the KAM Airways jet to Delhi early. The Kabul golf club visit made the trip. But first, upon retrieving my key at the hotel desk upon my return, I heard the two front desk attendants say, "Finally." Apparently, the Taliban agreed to endorse a three-day polio immunization project in the area under their influence via an Int'l Red Crescent/Cross 'letter of support.'

"Gee," I said, "Maybe there is a little good in all of us?"

"Yes, even the Taliban," the boys responded.

My thoughts immediately turned towards the cynical. A truce? If only three days? Why not launch a strike under the auspiciousness of the Red Cross Polio Project? I am quite sure they are also thinking the same thing? After all, it is a fucking war!

Room key in hand, I race to the room. Lips parched like after a three-hour camel ride in the Malawi desert. I drop everything on the still unmade bed, pull open the fridge door, and chug a 'Cool Blue' Gatorade in three gulps. Don't know if I've ever done that before. A beer in one gulp? Surely! (What is happening to my spelling?) Hell.

I have discovered what is wrong with the training program for the Afghani security forces! Pure and simple, they just want to dress cool like the private contractor security forces: club med sun glasses; fashionable long toed boots; western style baseball hats (not the same, drab, olive green one Fidel and Raul also wear).

After all, how can they go home with pride each night to younger brothers, sisters, girlfriends, wives, etc., if they are dressed like a Delhi elevator man? Let's give them a break. Build morality and let them choose their outfits from LL Bean, REI, or Abercrombie Fitch. I bet it will be one hell of a lot cheaper than the 'rag tag' collection of multi-war hand-me-downs we give them now.

And just think of the great PR/propaganda opportunities we're missing with garment tag branding and advertising. Think *Spiderman* or Harrison Ford, not *GI Joe*. I will have to wait until I get home to fully pursue this marketing opportunity, or what about the effect Hanna Montana or Miley Cyrus has? Home run!

Does it really make military sense to put a $5 million bounty on the head of someone we are stalking with an unmanned drone? Economic sense sure! But it seems just as ridiculous as a western sheriff showing his bravado by putting a five-hundred-dollar bounty on the head of Billy the Kid a month after the Kid died.

Enough of this literary crap! Forget last night and the night before! Forget the things I wasn't supposed to do, and more importantly, the things I was supposed to do. I'm turning on the fan, stripping to my underwear, opening another chilled Gatorade, popping three Tylenol PMs, a hand-full of generic water pills, and laying on the bed with today's *Afghanistan Outlook* newspaper. Friggin right! No one can see anyway, so maybe I didn't do it after all. Good Bye!

Okay Mona, I love the two-piece black, men's 'Perahan tonban.' Especially with a cream scarf.

Now, it's very important that I go back a few days worth of writing and make a sincere confession, and then clearly decide how to proceed with this travel journal! 'Nonfiction? Or Fiction?' Why? Because my previous words of that date were not only deceptive, but a literary lie! Not the first in publishing history I'm sure, but my first, and it just didn't set right.

Sunday night last, I was wrapping up an energetic and creative day of writing. It was getting late and I was finally getting sleepy when I realized a very easy 'short cut' had presented itself to me. *Why not? Who would ever know?* I pondered. Surely, I would never tell anyone! And they would never find out this, less than clever, ruse!

I know! Quit avoiding the issue. What happened Sunday night? Well, plain and simple, I got creatively frightened. I wasn't sure I could continue my writing at such a torrid pace the next morning. Hell, I might even forget some important things as the result of sleep. Or, the lack of it. So, I started to write about tomorrow that night. Even before the Kabul cock crowed or the next day's Ramadan sun had risen. Why not? All I had to do was make sure the 'new' literary tomorrow was exciting and it would be fine. Big mistake. Tomorrow was indeed one of the best and most interesting days of my life.

So, with forgiveness, I will write about yesterday tonight and explain the 'Chinooks.' Oh those frightful Chinooks and my 40-year-old memories. I wish they had never come back. Especially in this god forsaken place!

But first let me finish my 11X17 copy of the $10 Saturday's *WSJ* and listen to the first rains of the monsoon that followed me from Delhi in what seems like a month ago.

Damn you, Jim Brown, wherever you are! This afternoon, after a close 9-hole game of golf at the Kabul Golf Course, I had a great nap during which I dreamed about a relationship with an exotic Air India flight attendant. Then you showed up with my father's favorite ax. You told me to pack and that I would only be gone for 30 days, then you began to unpack. Dream or not, it did not bode well for my relationship. Thank God, when I woke up you both (and the ax) were gone and I was still here.

Ah, today is truly my hajj! The clouds have parted; the sun is shining warmly; my hawk has once again taken to flight; the doves are safely and silently nestled under the eave and above my door; the travertine walkway to the dining room shines with its early morning wetness; and I, much like Hansel and Gretel, leave wet, slippery foot prints behind me as I venture out. Regular at last!

Maybe there is more than 'meets the eye' to another fitful night's sleep! Maybe the discomfort during the night and the too telling dreams are rewarded by the next day's afternoon nap? Seems such, I think. And, awakening from the nap (hopefully during a thunder storm), all from the prior night seems forgotten. And right. A senior moment? My first?

Well, as usually accompanies any fit of elation for me is my predictable and near sufferable appetite for critical observation and cynicism. I do not relish taming such because it is a sure sign I'm happy — if only for a moment.

The Chinooks are back! Nothing cynical about them. Out to the balcony to watch. Listening is just not a choice with these prehistoric, mechanical 'birds of prey' still today. Whatever the day is? I will have to check the paper. Had a sensible breakfast of three boiled eggs, jerky, juice, toast, and cheese. Went to the one computer business center. Checked e-mails (520 new) and stopped at one from my dear friend and art collaborator Denise. Read the subject line 'same ol' shit." Not ladylike (or man for that matter), but it still was exciting to hear from her after three weeks. She and her family are dear to me. And she understands me like a sister. But, of course, not as well as sister Judy, in case she's listening. On the third page of a reply when the power went off. Kept typing because the generator seemed to have kicked in. Is it still called typing? Doubt it. Clicked send! Screen went blank. Temperature started to rise.

Anger loomed over the horizon in the form of a darkening sky. It approached as swiftly as yesterday afternoon's monsoon.

Stormed out the door and went to the front desk. Laughter and smiles immediately ceased. The silence was as loud as a tree cracking in the sub-freezing arctic north. Jack London surely knows this sound!

"Mr. Bob, are you angry?" I was asked.

Such a question caught me completely off-guard. I didn't immediately know what to say in response, so I simply smiled. How could I not? They were so caring for me during my recent illness. I considered my response for a second, and answered as truthfully as I dared, "Yes, very! But not for all day. Only for five minutes here. Now. And I will only be angry with you!"

This was, of course, preposterous. A second later, we could do nothing but laugh.

And then at me. "We Know. We heard you."

Oh, if I could only wish away such pending anger tantrums as easy as a packet of Wyler's kiwi strawberry flavored diet powder dissolves in my drinking glass each morning at breakfast.

I asked if the young boy was back from school yet. Was he working in the store now? Yes! And Yes! I like him and had given him twelve super duper solar calculators with music MP3 player USB charging ports for his classmates.

I trudged back into the compound towards the store. Mulling over the excuse that, yes, the power went off, but the computer still ran on the generator. But, the Internet connection didn't work. Thus, the e-mail could not be sent! (Dog-eating test. Cow wire analogy) Make sense? I suppose so. Still angry? Of course. More so now that I was alone. Want a drink? Sure! A Bloody Mary. Gonna get one? Not likely. Didn't even know where to find one.

I got to the extremely sheltered back of the compound where the store was located. Looked at the 20' walls and rolls of razor wire atop and wondered why the store was back here and with such protection. Maybe he was the newly and questionably re-elected President Karzi's son?

Whoever the hell he was, he wasn't here, and the store was still locked. I turned to go back down the long, windowless path to the courtyard when I heard it. The same horrible sound in any country of our auto infested planet.

The screeching, thumping, screaming, honking sound of accelerated steel hitting the 'dummy like' softness of a human body. Then the universal, but all too brief, silence and awes as the horns resumed their honking and the unfair cruelty of life continued. The cruelty is in the death, of course. But, more so than in just an individual's death. That can be swept away and easily forgotten once the remains have been removed from the street and given to some family. A family who had not yet had the time to bc mournful. For, it was just a few hours earlier they had sent this unsuspecting child off to school or to play. But, surely with a smile on her face and theirs.

Although I will usually accept a salving balm in any way, shape, or form, today this accident was not the right medicine to relieve me of my anger. It was much too sacred and powerful an elixir. The 'elixir' of life could not, nor should not be selfishly horded for use at some later date.

Then I returned to my room, closed the door and thought, I wish she (I wanted it to be a more sorrowful she) had been killed in an airplane crash and with me. Then maybe people would remember our passing longer, more intensely? Maybe not?

My diarrhea returned a short time later, and my thoughts returned to the unpleasantness of the Chinooks.

Just finished an article for my very favorite *Afghanistan Times* newspaper. Just barely finished, in fact, when the maid knocked. I opened the door, looked at the wrinkled face (more worn from labor than age), saw the maid in Kabul plastic purple 'Crocs', and knew it was indeed her. I had just conquered my first Afghani cultural miasma. Recognition from without a burqa. The "Crocs" were a much more effective and readily available recognition tool than any retina test the CIA had ever developed. Only one very serious problem, however, how do I tell my friends back in Boulder, Colorado (who invented and created the Croc) that, here in Kabul it was called the 'Gator' and sold on the streets along with an abundance of DVDs, CDs and old VHS tapes. Of course they know, and even find a street vendor photo of such complimentary aspects.

My printing (spelling) whatever, SUCKS!!! If I had to submit this leather, elegant but pleasantly worn, travel journal for publication, the publishers in any country would just shake their heads and shrug in total bewilderment. They would never be able to decipher in which language it was written.

My spelling, grammar, and punctuation sucks. Sister Mary Theresa, I hope you are not looking down at me now!!! But, then, how did Burton, Livingston, Lewis, and Clark get their damn journals published? Surely, it was not after submitting some untamed, unspotted, non-wrinkled, and sterile Mac word document! And, my contemporary, laptop gendering contemporaries be damned, I'm sure your overly convenient and trustworthy 'spell check' will bring you and your starched, unsoiled, press room inhabiting selves to your literary knees eventually. I can only hope. And, not a minute too soon either. Gee, it is nice to be happy again. I guess I will go seek out, once again Karzai's unknown son in the back of the compound bunkered store once again.

Anger? Depression? Hubris? Don't know what you're talking about. Must surely be someone else you've been listening to.

Tears for the little girl? Those in the Chinooks? Yes, they are uncomfortably seated just beneath the surface, waiting to disengage like so many unsuspecting troops dropped from the air into some distant battle.

I am not sure anymore if I can, or want to be a teacher! I seem to struggle with the fact that it takes others so long to learn what it also took me to learn so many years ago. But then, my dear mother speaks to me, "Bob, always remember, the sooner you help others achieve success, the sooner you also will be successful!" I sure miss her. But then, out of selfishness, denial, and addiction, I missed her even more greatly when she was still alive.

Mothers? Yes, fathers are to be loved also, but why does almost every college football player (when realizing they are on national TV) turn to the camera, smile, wave, and say, "HI Mom!" But then, I'm quite sure that perfumes on Mother's Day always outsold the ties of Father's Day in the time of yore! Mother's Day brunches vs. Father's Day BBQ's? No competition!

Apparently, I'm just not going to shut up today! Wow! A real 'Seinfeld' moment — and, in Afghanistan! Remember the 'pastry' episode? I do! I remember them all well. They travel with me wherever I go. Whether rich or poor, happy or sad, well or sick, I always want to be a 'Kramer.'

But, now back to good old George and the pastry. While at his fiancée's parent's party, George goes harmlessly into the kitchen to clear some dinner plates. Always hungry, just as Newman is always starving, he sees the remnants of a half-eaten crème puff. He looks over his shoulder and reaches into the garbage can to secrete this sugary morsel away. From whom? Even he doesn't know, just like the monkey at the Treetops Resort in Kenya who just feels it has to reach into your window and relieve you of your camera.

Damn near lost over that one! But, her later smuggling attempt did the job for me.

Back to George. Poised, secretive, ready to take a bite of the purloined pastry when the door swings open. He looks up startled, but still somehow manages to rationalize, "But it was above the rim!" to his future mother-in-law!

My Seinfeld moment? Just a few minutes ago, while fixing a canned, 'late' Afghani hot dog sandwich in my room. I looked down just as two of the wieners slipped out, fell to the floor, but fortunately bounced onto the tattered Persian carpet.

I was just rearranging the bread for an attack, had just bent over to grab the wayward franks when I saw her. At least her shadowy burqa looking fixedly through the window. Stunned and embarrassed, I turned and just shrugged. She just turned and the burqa began to disappear being led by the near silent footfall of her lavender 'Gators.' I really know how George C. felt that day also. Could I have ever made her understand, "but they bounced onto the carpet?" No, not in any language.

OK! Now before the rain and my afternoon 'courtyard' cigar, let's get back to the damn

Chinooks, or should I more correctly say, back to getting back to really getting back to the Chinooks?

OK! OK! One more minute please. I just spotted my Brit expat 'non-friend' going for my favorite chair. Damn him. Got to hurry. Maybe broken toes are too sore, but I must try to beat those damn spindly, venous, no calved, unstable, and pale ex-pat aging Brit legs to my chair. Off I go. Back in a minute to talk about the Chinooks.

Back in a minute is most likely what will not happen to my already tenuous UK publishing contacts. Off in less than the speed of light but rolling thunder…OK, here I am in the garden. Sitting in my second favorite cigar-smoking chair trying my best to not acknowledge his red-eyed, porcine stare. I sadistically wished for a Chinook to appear overhead, but at least heard and saw some aging Afghani Kam Airways jet soaring overhead. The bastard looked up also. Calm down, I told myself. After all, gin-fueled, pale, and sun-burned British expat! Goodbye another potential UK publishing contact. Our eyes finally met. Then his dropped towards my legs. I was sure the victorious asshole had counted each and every one of my limps as I approached in defeat. In fact, I knew he had.

We faintly smiled at each other, my ex nonbest" Brit expat friend and I. My smile was in cautious surrender. His was more of one who'd just ascended to the top of some Olympic podium and was ready to accept the gold medal to gleefully raise it above my silver one.

Our conversation started slowly. Carefully. He, speaking about what was surely nothing, while mine was certainly about everything. The line had clearly been 'drawn in the sand.' Or, rather in the RPG detonation-scarred lawn beneath us.

I struck first and hard. "Do you know what Eneke[9] the Ibo bird said many years ago?" I challenged. "It might have been hundreds of years ago, but it was a premonition about war in Afghanistan. And, the Taliban."

He shook his head in disinterest, but his dropping eyes gave away his interest as they fluttered helplessly to rise.

"I'm surprised you don't know?" I continued. "Eneke the bird says that since men have learned to shoot without missing, he has learned to fly without perching."[10]

The Brit only retorted, "What in the blimey hell does a bird know about the Afghan war? Especially an Ibo bird!"

Secretly, I could not have agreed more, but as unsure as my words seemed to be, I was quite sure the gauntlet had been laid down perfectly. I puffed on my cigar and waited for him to strike.

I waited for what seemed like indeterminable

---

[9] - the bird character from Chinua Achebe's book entitled, *Things Fall Apart.*

[10] - Things Fall Apart, Chapter 3, ISBN 0-385-47454-7 - "Eneke the bird says that since men have learned to shoot without missing, he has learned to fly without perching. People adapt to other people's learnings, particularly when the other person's learnings would harm you if you kept on your present course."

minutes as I watched with crossed eyes through the cigar glow receding towards my youthful and tanned, albeit from a sun booth, questioning face when he simply said, "Only the Brits and Kipling know about Afghanistan and its wars! After all, didn't Kipling say in 1869 that "even the British military with its 1,000 years of education failed to defeat one Pashtun armed with only a rusty, two-shilling silver musket?"

I suppose so, was my only thought. I knew I'd read that quote somewhere in the distant past, but didn't have the historical conviction to comment in agreement! "Maybe he did," I answered. "Maybe he did. I surely liked most of what Kipling wrote!"

His leaden eyelids began to close. His anemic right leg crossed his equally anemic left, and he only smiled. Once again victorious, only this time he was about to raise his gold medal well above my questionably silver one.

"Dear God, please do not let the foreign prayer calls from the local mosque dissuade you from coming to save me!" Then an even more pleading silent call, "Mom! Sister Mary Theresa! Where are you when I need you to help me defeat this Calvinistic prick?"

A clear 'strike three' against any UK publishing endeavor. But, I was not yet defeated. This was not a baseball game. I would turn it into a cricket match where three strikes did not count as a defeat, and the victory was often decided by a score in the 100s.

Saved at last from the USA-hating, 'over the hill' Brit expat in the ExOfficio shorts and dollar store 'Leave it to Beaver' t-shirt. Damn, I sure hated anyone who tried to dress noticeably younger than their age — and so unfashionably so.

Saved not by my mother's God, nor my mother, nor even Sister Mary Theresa, although she was my last resort for salvation. Saved not by any god at all in fact, but by the same wonderfully articulate, intelligent, and handsome un-African peace-keeping delegation that only two nights prior I had almost ridiculed, even racially profiled by setting my pen to paper.

"Come, Robert," they called in unison. "Robert #2 that is!" Of course I knew Robert #1 was back home somewhere in Nigeria, or was it Kenya? Didn't matter. I was just happy to sit with them to celebrate another day of their cherished Ramadan. "But only if you eat!"

They had been insulted that I did not eat with them the last time! They also did not see me continually clutching my sides under the table to see how really overweight I was. But tonight I would eat with them. KFC chicken from a red and white KFC bucket, watermelon, whatever. Because I knew that to eat with them would make me happy and cause me to laugh heartily — at no one's expense but our own. "Laughter in unison was good," they said later.

When I left, I, as well as they, were cold. Not

a NW 'football playing' fall chill, but a 'snow will soon be coming to Kabul' cold. No fan or open window tonight. I sure hope I sleep well and that my dreams are kind. I think they will be. They'd have it no other way for me! On to tomorrow!

At 5:00 a.m., whatever tomorrow this might be, I was awakened suddenly by loud knocks on the door. I did not really know who it could be. Too early for the call I anticipated. Certainly not an emergency from home. They didn't know where I was, but then neither did I most of the time.

I got up. It was chilly. Even the floor was chilled. I wrapped the top sheet about me. I had no blanket. My night desk friend greeted me. "Hello, Bob," was all he said as he turned to go back out in the pre-dawn cold. He handed me a folded note and then left.

I closed the door and crawled back into the warmth of my artificially warmed, two-threadbare-sheeted bed. I unfolded the letter and just stared. Although the words inscribed could only be described as elegant and beautiful, it surely did not read as such. For it was written in Pashto. Now I knew who the message was from; Ahmed, the Pashtun driver from the bird market who was to take me this day, along with his convoy, to the distant Lake Amir mountainous region but, at 8:00 a.m. not 5:15 a.m.

I dressed without showering and took the note with me to the lobby. Upon arriving, I was surprised to see Ahmed and another diminutive, scruffy bearded, but nicely dressed Pashtun seated on a sofa in the lobby. They, as well as the night desk boy, waved to me in a greeting which was much more smiles than apprehension. I sat down amongst them and listened carefully to the very few words Ahmed's friend spoke: "Mr. Bob, Ahmed has decided it is not a good day for you to go to the mountains of Amir Region." OK I thought, but why? He continued, "It is not safe to travel today! Look west tomorrow morning. To the highest mountain — you will surely see the first snow in the pass!"

End of conversation, surely! They stood in unison as did the desk boy. As they bowed and turned to leave, Ahmed laughed and muttered, "Besides, your shoes have no toes!" (as was later translated by the desk boy). Just before he joined in, but cautiously, "And, Mr. Bob, you not walk well. Remember we sometimes have to help you up the stairs to your room!"

Yes, regretfully, I did remember those embarrassing and impossible times.

I gave them each a scarf to take with them to keep warm. Scarves I had purchased in some glittering but soulless New Delhi shopping mall weeks ago. Scarves I would never wear out of respect for their customs. Scarves only purchased to later be given away as gifts. Somewhere along that infamous 'Road Less Traveled,' roads that were greatly sought by adventurous travelers the world over.

They carefully placed their cups of tea on the table before us. Tea that I thanked the desk boy for giving them; then I turned to the desk boy, smiling but quite dejected "Please fill their cups with more hot tea, and let them take the cups with them."

They were uncomfortable with this gesture, but took the cups with them as they exited from the lobby toward the sliding steel security doors and bunkers which welcomed their exit.

"But, Mr. Bob, what about the cups?"

"I must have dropped them," I said as I pulled a 500 Rupee note from my pocket and secreted it into his shirt pocket. "Whether I go on the convoy or not, they need to be warm when they go on their journey today!"

He smiled, understanding, and hopefully he understood me better that morning also.

I told him to awaken me in two hours for breakfast, then turned and hobbled in my 'toeless'[11] shoes towards my room. I will really never know if they meant I should not go to the mountains today, or should none of us? Never will know, most likely.

Returning to my room, I heard a very muffled ruffling of feathers from above. I looked up and saw four BB-sized dove eyes but not sound. They just stared as I pushed open the door. Their hooded lips only blinked once briefly and then they disappeared

---

[11] - Bob was forced to cut off the toes of his shoes because of his broken toes.

deeper into their nest above my door and under the eave. As I closed the door softly, I knew exactly what they were thinking. Lying down on my bed fully clothed, I thought as did they, about why Eneke, my new Ibo bird friend, hadn't come to warn me that the trip to the mountains to see the birds had been cancelled?

Well, I suppose Eneke was pretty busy wherever he was. But maybe, he had sent Ahmed's friend, Khalad, to tell me this message instead?

I laid down until awakened an hour and a half later by the day desk boy. I shed my 'convoy' clothes and headed to take a shower. Did all the correct preparations: moved T.P. out of holder to back of toilet, rolled the bath mat against the opening at the bottom of the bathroom door, stood aside as I turned on the shower spigots, adjusted the shower head so the leaky spray no longer gathered on the shelf where I kept my bathroom 'things', felt to see if the temp was warm enough, then really stepped into nowhere!

Dolf Lundgren in Rocky IV, I thought. He used this very same doorless, curtainless, and even 'stallless' soviet shower accommodation. Strange, I thought: the floor was flat. The drain hole was in the floor between my gnarled, black and blue but warming feet! Then how in the hell did I break four toes during the night last Sunday? I looked around, searching for some answer, relishing the heat and the steam. Then I saw it: the culprit of four nights past.

Just below the towel rack, which never seemed to ever hold a towel, was the humorous thing called a radiator. A Soviet-made radiator never-the-less. A rusted serpentine structure hid by my collection of rough, hanging, and most likely, Soviet leftover bath mats.

As the shower continued to warm me, I reach toward it; not impeded by any of the non-existent 'obstructions' as mentioned prior. The very same obstructions, that if present would have made this a real shower and the bathroom, a Western one at that.

I fiddled with the various adjustments and found that they were all welded shut. Poor bastard showering after me, I thought not forgetting about the warning of the "snow coming to the pass much earlier this year."

Then I saw it. I had just shut off the shower, grabbed the largest of the equally coarse bath mat/towels. I had only looked down now that the whole rusty radiator was visible. I looked down to look closer at the soldered temperature knob which I'm sure Dolf Lundgren would merely have forced loose with his Rocky IV strength. But, apparently not Rocky IV's strength.

There were numerous of them – blood spots – one even with a bit of flesh still attached. I know what you're thinking, "Why were they still there after at least 4 showers?" Well, you stupid readers, as any CSI professional would know, I simply did not shower every day (maybe), or was it because they were imbedded between the radiator grooves and away from any direct water spray from the shower?

Who gives a shit! The fucking Soviet-made radiator had broken my already match-stick brittle, alcohol-damaged toes.

They deserved to be defeated, but why in an Afghan hell did they not take their fucking rusty Russian-made radiators with them when they left — or the whole fucking bathroom for that matter?

As I lay down in the bed now warm and dry with 'the' sheet pulled up to my chin, I forgot about breakfast. I awoke with a start sometime later. How much time later, I did not know nor, did my Father's Rolex watch on my night stand later know. I had not wound it for some days now. The watch. My dad (as well as my Mom, of hers) was always so proud of that watch. Never wanted to spend the exorbitant cost of cleaning it as quoted by his local Runyan Jewelers. "Too damn much, Mr. Runyan!" he always responded to Runyan's only helpful inquiry.

"Doctor, maybe you should get it cleaned just once. After all, it has been nearly 40 years since Bob gave both you and Pat those watches."

"Nah," he replied and just kept on banking the balls into the pockets in the pool hall of the Elks Club which was just over the Runyan's Jewelry store on Main Street, Vancouver, WA. "Nah, it still runs just fine!"

I would never have guessed that just a few, much too few years later, both Dad and Mom would be gone. But, their (my) watches would remain here and now carefully engraved with one lying on the table beside me in the bunker hotel in Kabul, and the other (most likely not ticking either), lying in an old silver Nambe' bowl beside my desk back home.

I listened from my bed and thought, *must be tomorrow already for sure. I had better get up, get dressed and check out the mountain pass to the East as previously instructed.*

The excess of bunker "mates" milling about the lobby immediately told me something was amiss. I soon found out it certainly was!

"You slept right through it old boy," (you know who) said. "You most certainly did." He went on to reiterate and, in the process, obtain that wonderful opportunity to ridicule an American amidst the certain support of his countrymen and, of course, women.

I grabbed the paper (Afghan Times) from his hands. Saw the date. Realized it was still today (although much later) 3:00 p.m. to be exact, but at least not yesterday or even tomorrow.

"I guess I did sleep through it," I said. "Whatever 'it' was."

"Surely you must know by now," he insisted. "Surely, even you whose people love war but aren't so bloody good at it anymore!"

I had had way too much of this bullshit by

now. I just wanted to sit and read the paper and savor a cold Diet Pepsi, or Pepsi Light as it was more commonly called here in this anything but common land.

He had me cornered on the couch by now as he continued. The unusual amount of other Western workers had most likely had their fill of his banter by now and were all silently grouped around the lobby's large (but not flat) screened Sanyo television I glanced over to my 'ex best', no, expat friend and just listened in surrender.

Then, everyone gasped and put hands to their faces or rubbed them with unmanicured and cracked nails, through their hair. These were the UN and NCO hands that were really trying to change Afghanistan for the best. These are the same well-worn and knowledgeable 'mitts' that won title fights, and once 'brought home the bacon!' These were the illiterate but oh so articulated hands with fingers that the soldiers' rifles (on both sides) fought for.

"Nearly 30 dead today around Kabul and Western Afghanistan. 16 US troops in 'here, there, and here again' while eight British troops were killed here in the capital when a UN convoy they were guarding was struck by insurgent's and two IED's early this afternoon just a block away from the USA Embassy."

So that is what I had slept through?

What they so dearly fearfully awaited hearing.

Then it continued and now we were ALL transfixed to the TV with the announcer from the BBC standing just before the smoldering wreckage of a car. Black, oily smoke billowing up towards my birds and the soon-to-be extreme upper elevation of the 'highest pass' still well beyond. Clouds, cries, smoke, sirens, but no kites. This must truly be bad? There was almost always a kite somewhere in all televised newscasts. The kite, like the ever-present finger smudges on my screen(s) back home. There before us every day, they, not to annoy, but rather to remind us that yes, no matter how important the news, there was always something more important to clean that day whether it be finger prints off the TV screen or the toilet bowl in a bathroom.

The smudge was most likely one of the only times the televised smudge was truly competing with what was on screen! Or, was it just me? The anal retentive, obsessive-compulsive freak that I was, who had to vacuum the footprints out of the carpet each night before he went to bed only to replace them with more (unsteady) footprints early in the AM when he sought out the 'first drink' of the day. 'Hair of the dog they always called it.' I liked that! Maybe the fucking 'dog' they always referred to made all those damnable early A.M. footprints in the carpet between my bedroom and my study.

I never had a den, only a study, and I did not need some Elizabethan study in which to drink. Any old study would serve the purpose of my drunkenness well. 'Elizabethan?' Yes, back to my bunker mates from the UK and 'him!'

The airport is closed. The green zone is off limits to anyone who did not live and/or work there. An excellent preventative policy in any event, I surmised.

The road to the airport is closed! Now, for football results brought to you by 'whatever' bank!

The 'Telly' was switched off just a moment before they all started to recede back into their jungle compound. Confused and saddened, I too left, but not before one (sure to not be a final one) on this abruptly ending afternoon.

"If we return to the jungle, we'll dress for dinner."[12]

The breeze was soft and cool that night. The fan was not necessary. Besides, it did not induce sleep anyway. It only muffled the sounds from without that I blamed for not inducing sleep, when those sounds on the inside were much more disturbing.

One sheet was fine. As was a prayer. My first of the trip. In fact, just maybe the first of my sober life — and best of all, this was not a prayer asking God or anyone else for anything. I was merely offering thanks to my two Pashtun friends and surely warriors, no matter which side they were on, in this Rubik's cube of a conflict.

I simply told them I loved them and would

---

[12] - The Drowned World, J. G. Ballard, Chapter 3

never call any of their people 'rag heads' again, for I truly believed that they (with the help of my Ibo friend Eneke) saved my life this day. I really do not believe anyone else had done such. Maybe they had wanted to try to save me in the past, but I surely never let them. I fell asleep knowing full well now that Eneke was my sister Judy. The tears came ever so slowly that night and crashed upon my unsuspecting cheeks with a thunderous sound which could only be compared to the seventh incoming wave preceding a winter storm on the Oregon coast. Just like the wave, my tears will also run their course but (hopefully) only to return someday when I have reason to offer the second prayer of my sobriety to other than myself.

"Good morning, Kabul," as Adrian Cronauer would have said. Just noticed the elegant charcoal-colored script adorning the 'Khayam' light fixture in the bathroom. Yes, that very same 'John', 'outhouse', or 'crapper' that was an integral feature in the set design of 'Rocky IV or damn it, was it III, or, God forbid, even V? No, not V. That was only just made, I believe, or was it Rambo V that was to be made? Whatever, who in the hell won Super Bowl IV or V anyway? Could it have been Sly Stallone? I know it was not Joe Namath. Although he did have white athletic shoes like me, but if I remember those many years ago watching the game on a rainy Monday in my Dad's den, Joe's (Broadway Joe's) white shoes had toes! Maybe it would have been OK for him to go into the Almir mountains with the convoy yesterday — I wonder. But, then I sure seem to spend an inordinately large amount of time just 'wondering' these days. Oh well, time for a shower!

What is the true story about 'Marjan the Lion?' Isn't the phrase 'I'm sorry' in a greeting card an oxymoron?' Got just such a card left at my door this a.m. from 'un clair' from county Cork! Yes, Mother, she has beautiful red hair. Mother, I will not ask her out on a date. I promise. Oh, what wonderful annual trips to her motherland. I eventually accompanied her because she became too old to rent a car anymore, and maybe it just might have had something to do with the Esso gas station she crashed into with the rental on her last trip to the island. Her island. Our island. Much as Cuba was ours to share also. Eightieth birthday cigar dinner with the guy, Mom and Fidel. Enough!!!

Got to the lobby this day (their holiday) (not a holiday but a day off!) to find the place nearly deserted at 11:00 a.m. Forgot that Friday was everyone else's (but mine) Saturday. Of course, I did not forget. After all, why else had I prearranged a driver to take me to the Kabul Zoo where the famous Afghan lion, Marjan,[13] once lived. I was still going to pay tribute to this 'King' of the (anything but jungle), hard scrabble land: 'Marjan, defender of all defenders against the Taliban.'

I am sure Eneke knows Marjan. Maybe something that happens today will let me know for sure! One never knows about such things, do they?

---

[13] - Marjan was a lion in Kabul Zoo who suffered a hand grenade attack by the brother of a man that Marjan had killed. See the following link: http://www.lionlamb.us/lion/marjan.html

Checked at the desk about my car. "Mr. Bob, problem. Car won't be here for an hour." Okay, I'll just read the paper in the lobby and wait. Maybe my latest 'letter to editor' will appear in today's Post.

Then, just prior to sitting down, I felt a pinch around my waste. A painful pinching at that indeed. (see, I am trying to write more like the Brits now to possibly lure back the non-existent UK publishing contacts I may (yes, certainly did) have alluded to in previous pages. Oh well, back to the 'pinch.' I wonder if Seinfeld ever had an episode called 'the pinch?' Don't think so because I'm pretty sure I've seen them all numerous times 'prior.' (Don't overdo the Brit thing, Bob!)

Anyway, if it was anything like my 'pinch' it would have been a great and memorable episode with George C., the definite 'fall guy!' The 'pinch' was nothing more than the pressure from my nearly depleted money belt pressing against a new found weight, a most certainly unwelcomed 100kg exactly. Actually I would never have known how to convert pounds like that except we all knew, growing up as I did, a kilo of 'stash' was always 2.2 lbs. Sister Mary Theresa, wouldn't you be proud of me knowing this? But then, I was never 'one of them' but only a professional drinker, as a scornful judge once so labeled me. I knew also that one meter was equal to 39.37 inches. Why? Because like Mark Spitz, I used to swim. But he, the freestyle, and I, the crawl. Actually raced him once.

"Mr. Bob! Mr. Bob," shouted the desk boy. "There is another bomb somewhere, so the traffic will be bad for another two hours."

"Okay," I replied. I thought a moment and then praised his wonderful optimism about there being only one bomb and a two-hour (more) traffic delay. I went back to my room to write a brief story for Monday's Peace Day when today turned out to be 'peace day' after all. At least between me and my new Brit, expat friend. His calling out the window as I passed startled me for many reasons.

I glanced at the clock. 3:00 p.m. No taxi. Down the stairs I go and across the abandoned courtyard to reach the front desk to be told, "Only one hour more wait, Mr. Bob." No more waiting for me and my sore but anxious '10 dogs.' Nope. I was fully suited up in my journalists' attire. We surely all knew what that same predictably drab outfit looked like. If not, just remember that ass Geraldo Rivera kneeling in the sands outside of Baghdad in 2001 giving away his position and that of the troops he was embedded with for all of CNN and thus all the world to see.

Or, take the always poised and mysterious Christiane Amanpour. For she, above them all, wore the vests, cargo pants, and only semi-revealing, multi-pocketed shirt (underneath) with not only grace but the presence of mind to know she would someday have her own interview televised show (9/21/09 Peace Day) premier.

Ah, but the 'Scud Stud' (Rivera) never dressed in this utilitarian Middle Eastern 'war at the front' fashion. No, he wore a sheepskin collared leather bomber jacket while on the roof of some long forgotten (and surely) rebuilt Baghdad hotel as he reported the great successes of the 'shock and awe' being illuminated behind him.

Damn, Mom loved everything about this guy. Not the war, surely for she had already been in one in Vietnam (1968), and had seen her husband (Dad) depart for another (1942).

No, but the 'Scud Stud' was a true reincarnation of her beloved William Powell!

Down the steps I go. Through the huge sliding steel security doors, past the first sand-bagged bunker where I dole out a few dollars to the sleeping (but not yet snoring guards), then out a small door past another street-side guard bunker (no tips here because the guards were off somewhere else) and onto Chicken Street!

Great day of disoriented walking. Most often paced by numerous street urchins seeking a rupee of sustenance. Some even clever enough to mimic my limping gait as they strode beside me as so many frogs, but with a streetwise hand always open. Arms extended hoping to better position themselves for an alm! No luck for them, however. My years of globetrotting had taught me that even to offer only the most simple, crumpled and dirty Rupee just lit off an emergency 'flare' of possibility for the other street-wise dregs.

Signs flashed by with only a few words recognizable. Such as 'Morri's very best Curtains.' Horns honked ceaselessly.

Reaching the ultra-deluxe Five-star Hotel Serena, I passed through three very secure and bunkered positions and one final body scan before being allowed into the lobby. But, nothing really new to me. I smiled, remembering the times I had come here prior to purchase day-old copies of the *New York Times* and the *Wall Street Journal*, but I'd never approached by foot. Approaching as a Westerner with car and driver was much simpler, I thought. But, not nearly as much fun I realized as I reached into my Velcro half-closed vest pocket and felt the handle of my jungle survival (surely tested — at least the box said so, but by whom?) knife and realized it had made it through three security scans to be revealed in x-rays as only a camera.

After a few moments of air-conditioned relaxation (the weather had suddenly turned hot and dusty again outside), I got up to venture out onto Chicken Street. Only this time following the late afternoon sun west toward the daily prayer calls and the darkness that would signal the end to another chaste and proud day of Ramadan.

As I returned to the street, embraced by only a very sketchy experience of just moments ago heading East on Chicken Street, the mini, doe-eyed Oliver's attacked me. Free from the bonds of some

Dickensonion Fagan who most surely lurked in the hovel of their 'off street' warren, and coaxing them onward with nary a command or glance. No, the sea of starving urchins was propelled by something much more than greed or a fear of the 'Fagan.' They were motivated to a frenzy by the need to please, the need to eat, the need to sleep safely, Off the street and in the comfort of their mingled, rag-covered arms and limbs — much like me, they just did not want to sleep alone, if only for one other night.

I bid them a kind adieu as I entered a closet-sized sidewalk restaurant named *Milano* (Pizza Express) (accordion airplane bathroom size). Of course, why would I eat anywhere else? I'm quite sure all of the non-existent travel guides will surely have included it. That is, if and when, they ever did exist!

Anyway, I perused the cracked plastic, bent cornered, tri-fold menu before me. I was surprised. The offerings did not look bad at all. While the two waiters in the matching and, most likely 'pirate branded' green, short sleeve, *Sprite* t-shirts, stared at me, I pondered the culinary selection. Finally I ordered a Coke Light. One's immediate answer was "NO!"

"Okay," I replied. "A Diet Pepsi?"

"NO!" was the other's response.

Then I boldly went down the menu, but hesitantly asked, "Fanta?"

"Sure," came the reply from the first waiter.

He reached behind my chair and opened the lid of an old-fashioned cooler, picked out a cool, moist, and dripping can of Fanta, and plopped it down in front of me. I received no glass, no straw, nor a napkin with which to mop up the increasing flood of water on the table.

I moved forward so the very well-coiffed, traditionally dressed, middle-aged gentleman squatting behind my chair could continue to Q-tip clean the retro chrome bars of my chair and the other two matching ones at the table.

Moving on and forward. So the very well coiffed, traditionally dressed middle-aged gentleman squatting behind my chair, could continue to Q-tip clean the retro chrome bars of my chair and the other two matching ones at the table.

No, not cleaning in such a detail-like fashion that every car buff, including Leno, would seek him out to 'powder puff' and classic wax one of their vintage autos. He continued with his labors, not sweating, but surely putting Monk, Felix Unger, or even myself to sanitary shame.

Just as I was about to flag down one of the waiters, a bell rang and the door opened. A very western dressed Afghani family entered. They looked at me, and then asked the host, the other of only two lads in green t-shirts, something I could not hear. They nodded, of course in unison, as they all do and left. *No big deal*, I thought and waved the menu towards the waiter. He started to approach my table when the bell rang once more and another family entered. Even the squatting, potential IED setter by my chair looked up this time. Popular place, I thought.

Proud of my non-guide-book culinary section, but before the applause — self-congratulatory of course — had settled in the exact manner as the first. I immediately felt guilty and was just about to perform the dietary bane of the west: 'cross ordering', when a voice from below said in perfect English, "Are you ready to order, sir?"

"Yes, yes," I replied.

As he now stood before me he pulled an official order pad from the pocket of his muslin (not Muslim, stupid) tunic and placed the pen cantered ever so slightly before him and waited.

I suddenly felt rushed and uncomfortable as the lines of items, from 1 to 60, blurred and seemed to involuntarily pass before me like an up and/or down escalator. I focused on a selection just as he said, "No Pizza! We are out of pizza until 6:00 pm."

After Ramadan, I supposed. No matter to me however. "I will take #4, the mushroom-garlic soup and #51 the chicken club sandwich."

"Great," he said and walked away.

I was now hungrier than ever watching the sun begin to sink towards the western horizon which was the ancient fort on the top of the hill before me. Yes, much more energy would be needed shortly if I was to navigate home successfully before darkness.

I ate a great meal. Paid the reasonable bill ($5 USD), left a 100 AFS tip and left the place with a proffered souvenir 'take out' menu in my left breast pocket. Turning right, I immediately lumbered along, but with more haste, West on the non-commercial side of Chicken Street. The evening sun drenched the non-commercial north side of Cricket Street in fact.

I say 'lumbered' out of no disrespect to any other impedimentally challenged individual such as myself — not even the professionally maimed Dickensonian street lurching, for we all know very well that the bear also 'lumbered', but was also capable of a speed up to 60 km per hour when startled and put to flight.

Onwards I went. Sideways at times. Backwards at other times. Nearly downwards on other occasions and often times, hesitantly upwards. Over pot holes and curbs, stones and limbs — the tree kind, of course — but never, seemingly, forwards. I began to worry somewhat. Not really about my safety, but more about my constant disorientation and inability to even ask for the most simple direction (US male stereotype intact by now surely). There was also the rapidly impending, or quite more so, darkness — a chilly, Kabul wartime darkness — a forbidding darkness which only got darker as the electricity failed — more often than just on an occasion, mind you. A frightening and numbing darkness in which only a blind man could see.

I retraced my steps a few short blocks and hurried in yet another of what I had previously considered to be the right direction. I was immediately and thankfully rewarded by the glint of the sunlight receding behind the fort as it sparked like some aging firefly. Only for a second did it guide me from its perch atop the construction crane which was atop the roof of the Dutch Embassy. Only two blocks from home. I congratulated myself and only myself since I had already forgotten that final burst of light from the 'sun's firefly' or was it from Eneke?

I didn't take time to wonder any longer, however; I was afraid to wonder anymore and possibly realize that one of Eneke's favorite foods back home might be the firefly.

I entered the compound and relaxed to the welcome onslaught of my *bunker mates'* many questions and inquiries, all with genuine concern; it was something that would most likely frighten me later that night, much more than the dark.

A lady then stopped me in the hallway.

"Bob, you seem very intellectual," she stated. She was with the UN from Holland. I noted no little wooden shoes on her feet or windmills dancing in her eyes though.

"I guess so," I answered. "Not smart, but yes, intellectual in a 'hazmat' sort of way!"

Her brows furrowed over those tulip blue and

white eyes.

"I mean, at any moment, I may self-destruct, intellectual or otherwise," I continued.

She didn't like this conversation, so she invited me to her compound room where, I am certain she felt much more secure.

I watched her slowly, and most carefully, sip her South African Riesling wine from the bottle before refilling her glass. She was right, of course; I knew she was, but I never had to say it. I left her room an hour later removing her lipsticked and toothpaste-stained wine glass from her hand as she slept. I liked her very much, and if only for a moment, wondered if I would also sleep well beside her?

Ascending the not yet lit stairs to my room, I paused, if only for a second, to reflect upon something Sally Field said to an adoring Academy Award audience which had just bestowed upon her an Oscar. She said, to much later ridicule, "I feel it...and I can't deny the fact that you like me! Right now! You like me!" Well, tonight I realized my bunker mates cared about me, and maybe, just maybe, loved me! I lay in bed, the fan turned on high, it was sure to be a restful sleep — but not right now, the sounds of frivolity and drunkenness emanating from the next room so correctly predicted.

"Robert! Robert!" I heard pleadingly through my cracked open window only moments later.

"Robert, you must come join us. We are having such fun!"

I considered joining them, remembering the many nights in the past when I stayed home alone drinking to excess — alone because it allowed me the nonjudgmental right to attain another night of drunkenness — a night which I would soon regret. Just like all those other nights so wantonly scattered before me like the shards of broken bottles that always seemed to litter the same path behind me, but never the 'not yet taken' path before me.

"Robert! Robert! I am going to come and get you. I know you are just pretending sleep!" Yes, that most vociferous Belgian of their lot was right, Oh how I wished I really had the power to, if only feign, sleep when I so wanted it, I thought as I got up, turned on the bedside lamp, and pulled on my shorts just before exiting my room for the room across the hall.

I left them a short time later. Much too soon for them, but not for me. In fact, just as the 'American baiting' had begun.

"Robert, you will never understand things here. You think just like an American; whereas we have a European thought about such things!"

"Maybe," I said as I turned to leave. "But I am not all that sure that the Afghanis feel the same."

After all, what did they, in that room, really know about America? They had most likely never visited the place on vacation or to study. I remained silent, ignoring their further tauntings. I closed the door politely recalling what my dear friend, Fidel, had once said in a Havana court room in 1954, "History will absolve me!"

I entered my much-needed period of slumber not angry at them or anyone for that matter. Maybe they were right. Maybe I was right or, maybe there was really no right. Maybe that was why we were all so incorrectly here in Afghanistan. I remembered one failed attempt to 'fluff' my unfluffable — what must certainly be a Russian — pillow. Then, I no longer remembered anything anymore at all.

The social life for non-Afghanis in Kabul can honestly be compared to a floating crap game. The 'dice' of new social introductions and farewells just keep rolling day after day, month after long month. Both within and without their risk-taking, gambling with life anyway, compounds. The biggest loss? Social disenfranchisement or more simply, the eventual loss of one's new and necessary 'best friend.'

I looked into my desk drawer for the first time and found a nesting coil of 'pre-USB' technology that was most likely left over from the installation of the soviet radiators, or very similar to my own lower kitchen tool drawer, full of cables, cords, and never-sent-in warranty cards and registration forms. All of it carefully coiled and awaiting that one definite day in my very *indefinite* future when I will learn to use them — that time in the future when they will be rendered even more technologically obsolete than they all are now. But then, one never really knows when the red/white color-coded cables that once connected my Betamax to my TV might become useful again.

Visiting Marjan

I woke up Saturday very happy. Not because it was Saturday, but because this was going to be the Saturday when I would go to the zoo to see where Marjan lived, or more correctly, where he once lived as the bravest lion in Afghanistan and quite possibly, the bravest lion in the world!

Yes, I said *when!* not *if.* I had an overabundance of confidence in my negotiating skills, the weather seemed right (no snow in the pass, ha ha) the traffic would be better, and I was sure the Taliban were resting from their last cowardly and fatal attack on Kabul.

Yes, again for more emphasis only, not the lack of another 'positive sounding' word, the planets, or as the Afghani writer Housenni (think the kite flyer) would have said, 'Suns.'

I took a hasty shower, got dressed in comfortably clean adventure wear, and prepared to be transported to some distant part of the city where I was told there was an old rundown zoo with only about 100 hungry birds and animals living there. Not a pretty or fun place (yeah, like the Kabul golf course, I'm sure) but still a fun place the young boys and girls loved to go on Fridays to meet each other beyond the range of social and/or religious scrutiny of their elders.

After all, hadn't the 19-year-old desk boy invited me to join him yesterday, and wasn't he truly dejected when I said only, "Maybe." Well, feeling and looking great, I headed out the door and almost bowled over my "no name" room attendant. She was standing on my door mat, only partially burqa'd (I could see her eyes, brows, and almond-colored cheeks for the first time). Wow! She was damn near in a bikini! Oops, Bob, be careful here. Remember where it got your old buddy, Salman Rushdie?

Anyway, she was just standing on my mat and staring at the repulsive and insulting (to her anyway, and yes, to me also, I had to admit) She stood with her covered arms precariously balanced on her hips shaking a little and I am sure not smiling. How did I now know? I could see the most expressive parts of her (anyone's for that matter) face. Well, I got a little 'harmlessly' ahead of myself here. I was still peering from an only partially opened door and wondering what was keeping the door from opening completely.

Finally, she moved, bent to reach her cleaning basket, turned to look at me (ha! see!), did not smile nor was it a frown, and only left to my cheerful "good morning." Then I saw it. The scattered and want-only discarded remains of 'their' last night's revelry, or as they rationalized, 'just another night in the compound celebrating just another day of Ramadan!'

Gee, was I led to believe that once Ramadan officially ended, their revelry would cease? Naw! Mine never did. I thought of the awaiting Marjan as I nudged the wine bottles, beer cans, airline shot bottles, and half-full food containers aside with, yes, my open toed shoes. Then, I still just didn't feel all that good about leaving my little lavender imitation Croc-wearing friend with all this hurt. I got my own garbage bag from my room and hastily filled it with their (anything but party-like) debris. Yes, hastily! I surely did not want to have anyone see me and be frightened by my (although meaningful) attempt to disrupt the disorder of their ordered system much like Robert Heinlein's *Stranger in a Strange Land*.

Now, where do I put this crap? Who gives a shit? I thought and dumped it before my now closed room door, washed my hands with a sani-towel (which I threw on top), and went down the stairs to breakfast on my way to visit the ghost of the brave one-eyed, Taliban fighter lion named Marjan.

Breakfast was just breakfast as it was every day of the week. Never a bit bland nor a selection of food stuffs you could ever mix in the hopes of making it more interesting than yesterday, today, or even tomorrow — and due to the bespeckled Asians eating around me, I never enjoy breakfast or them or any other damn meal they eat with their rudely bowed heads, 90 degrees to the plate, early morning gnarled, and hair hanging in their eyes, and just safely above their 'never stop moving' knives, forks, or spoons. Then, spearing the intended food item, raising their heads in a horizontal fashion only to return to looking at their plate and the food item they next planned to quite emotionally ram into their throats just like so damn many of their sacred and fetid dragons.

Meal time conversation? Hardly with a Westerner while here in Kabul. Damn, I hate their uncaring and self-righteous manners just like the over hurried pace of their wooden two-inch heeled shoes passing regularly in an obnoxious (at least bronze medal) pace.

Ah Ha! The driver was there waiting when I re-entered the lobby from the breakfast room. The very same gun toting security guard become driver whom everyone said 'really wanted to take Mr. Bob to the zoo.' The very same zoo to which no one went. Especially foreigners. A zoo so wanton and desperate that it was really only the destination for young people so damned desperate for a cultural and spiritual respite from their elders that it seemed like a Garden of Eden to them. It was to this very zoo that my driver and I sped that early Saturday morning.

It is always nice to recognize a really adventurous outing when it is beginning. Mine surely was as we shook, rattled, and rolled in a cloud of Afghani dust towards Kabul, past hills (with palatial homes/pools) and dales (not so palatial). In fact, hobbit-like dwellings crowded there (or should I say honey-combed) much like the ancient monk's cave dwellings Mom and I saw carved into the ancient hillside cliffs of old Salzburg when we visited for my 50th birthday for the international music festival. Prearranged box seats with the King and Queen of Norway, not Babe Ruth or Lou Gehrig box seat quality, however.

We screeched to a halt. I didn't know one's auto could come to a screeching halt on dirt, dust, and pebbles, but we did, thank you! We stopped before what appeared to be nothing but a blue outhouse-sized box with a window in it and a hand jutting from the windowless window.

Everyone seemed to know what to do. Everyone but me, that is. But then, 'everyone' was only the driver, me, the man collecting the money, and a wizened old man leaning on a very damaged alabaster lion statue. The driver paid, he gave the tickets to 'lion man' $1.50 for both, and we entered a very nondescript blue archway only to be greeted by the most wondrous bronze, warm statue of Marjan.

Oh, and quickly so as not to lose my train of thought (ya, sure Bob, as if there ever was one), there were two others when we approached. The man and boy who washed cars. Thus, no surprise at the lack of AK-47 type crowd control.

"Marjan, the Lion," I whispered, laying a

trembling hand upon the forehead of the statue. "How great it is to finally see you after all these years."

Strange it is how a tear trickled from my eye, meandered its way down my roughened and red cheek, finally to disappear into the gray beard of this humble and hobbled old man as he stood before the Hero of Kabul.

I immediately sat on a blue bench in the shade nearby and wrote the following story. I dedicate it now to the memory of Marjan, to myself, to the commemoration of Peace Day, and most of all, to the spirit of the Afghani people, which lives in all of us who love freedom!

Marjan, the Greatest Lion of Them All

"In a land far, far away called Afghanistan, there lived a great lion. His name was Marjan."

All the people said the brave Marjan was neither afraid to go into the high, snow-covered mountains or to the barren and hot sandy desert.

But the people were not completely surprised at Marjan's strength and bravery because they were a strong and brave people also.

It was not so long ago that a strange people came down from the North.

They did not arrive to help the brave people of Afghanistan, they came to subdue them. Whenever Marjan sniffed the air, he smelled the danger brought by these new people, and he smelled the evil desire in their hearts.

On one particular night around a

very big fire, Marjan and the people listened to their elders. They listened carefully, for the news was not good.

Although the news was frightening to hear, the people and Marjan remained unafraid. They listened to the words of the elders and knew what they had to do. There was to be a fight for their religion, their country, and their way of life.

They were to do battle with a mighty and terrible foe, but they had the mighty and terrible Marjan to lead the brave forces against the enemy in the North lands. The elders, on the other hand, would lead the people throughout the other provinces in the south, and in Kabul itself.

The fighting lasted many long years before the enemy was defeated and driven back to their land to the North with many fewer people than when they arrived. The people of Afghanistan were very weary and bruised from all the fighting, but they were victorious and held a great celebration to honor those who had given their life for their freedom and the right to live the way they chose to live.

Marjan, himself, was weary after the long war. Now much older and whiter, but still very brave, he mysteriously chose to remain in the Northern mountains with his soldier friends.

Everyone throughout Afghanistan very much missed Marjan and his great warrior stories, but there was peace now across the land to be appreciated.

In time, the people forgot about Marjan and returned to the life they had lived for hundreds of years before.

Then one day the people looked around and saw a horrible new enemy coming at them from every direction. For the first time, these brave people were very afraid. It was then that they recalled brave Marjan. The people called out in prayer for Marjan to return to the south lands.

Marjan, however, was very busy with another war in the North. A very new and strange war. He did not hear the people call to him in prayer.

For many years, the strange enemy fought the people — an enemy who was of the people themselves. Marjan finally heard about this terrible new enemy. He did not like Afghans fighting Afghans, so he came down from out of the north mountains to talk to all of the people.

He arrived in Kabul with the elders in the middle of one very cold and dark night. No one saw them arrive because they came in the middle of a beautiful white snowstorm.

The next day, though, many people met with Marjan and the elders as they had done so many years ago. Only this time the people did not listen. They only yelled at each other and argued. Marjan was saddened by this because he really wanted to love all of the Afghan people, but there was no longer anything he could do.

With great sorrow, Marjan and the elders prepared themselves to enter another snowstorm and head back to the North. But before they could do so safely, a man ran up to Marjan and offered him some candy. Marjan accepted, but when he bit into the candy, it exploded with great fire and smoke.

Marjan, the brave and strong lion, did not die that day. He never understood the reason why the man gave him the exploding candy either. Instead, he lived many more years with love in his heart. He even forgave the man who had hurt him.

Over time, though, hearing about all the sadness throughout the land, he became very sick and even more worried about the people and their future. When he did finally die, he died peacefully in a non-peaceful land, in a warm room with his Afghan friends caring for him to the end.

Marjan died sad, however, wanting peace for all the people of Afghanistan.

So, whenever you think of Marjan, smile warmly and think of peace for all. "Happy Peace Day!"

The End

I found myself very tired after two hours of writing on the blue bench in the zoo. So tired in fact that I was silent in the car on the way back to the hotel. We passed the bustling, old city open markets that line the Kabul River, went past the ancient mosques, the Presidential Palace, and the 500- year-old bird market which I no longer wish to visit after I learned they have bird fights there on Saturdays. Past the very evil-looking Interior Ministry Building and prison, but then were they not supposed to look evil to instill fear in the people and keep order in the land? At least everyone I had ever seen, and most assuredly the ones I had the grave misfortune to *visit,* had appeared that way, no matter in which nation they actually resided.

I thought of Guantanamo, a place I had personally seen from both Cuba and US-occupied

Cuba. And then, of course, there was Abu Ghraib which served as a waterproof match to the tinderbox of this whole damned mess anyway.

Back at the hotel, I picked up my room key and hobbled back back to my cozy room (#126) to be alone with Marjan and our thoughts — to rest, and maybe find some early sleep. It was still light and the last day of Ramadan was still to rise. I read an article entitled, *Wal-Mart on Christmas Eve Day*. I have thoughts regarding it, but I will keep them to myself. I'm feeling a bit selfish at the moment.

Sleep went well. Well, that is after I was able to 'digest' one looming failure in my past. What does the 104-year-old Gregorio Fuentes (Hemingway's Old Man and the Sea) have to do with Kabul's Marjan the lion? I'm not sure you could have guessed what, but here is the 'pre-sleep' 'pre-EID' holiday answer, my patient friends.

In the early morning of January 13th, I received a collect call from Cuba. I answered it only to find out that my 104-year-old friend Gregorio Fuentes had passed away. The family in Cojimar, Cuba wanted me to 'break the news to the world.' Quite an honor, but I had watched over Gregorio for nearly 10 years by that time. They wanted me to call the Reuters News Service which I surely did.

I made immediate plans to leave for Cancun/Cuba with Val, who, by that time, had become extremely close to both Gregorio and his grandson, Raphael, as well. We were forced to cancel those plans, however. We were too late. We discovered that the Cuban government did not possess proper refrigeration equipment to store the body. Thus, the family was forced to bury Gregorio in the afternoon on the same day of his death. Within days, the government seized the house. Within months, it was shuttered and boarded up. It distressed me greatly, but there was little I could do about it. What does any of this have to do with Marjan or me being an alcoholic? Just listen a little longer, please.

Almost every addict, recovering or otherwise, carries with them a well-used colander in which to place unfulfilled dreams and dreams which will certainly never be realized. False ambitions, well-meanings, and other such 'nonsense' rattle around noisily and quite visibly for all the world to see before they are flushed out through the holes of the alcoholic's 'colander' like oh so many before them.

Why in hell didn't I feel that my mere attendance in Cuba was sufficient? It was very expensive to travel to that country, and as if that wasn't enough, it was quite illegal to do so. Well, you can quit guessing. It just wasn't sufficient to me.

When I did finally get down to visit Gregorio's family some months later, I was treated as family, much to the curiosity of the International Press. But why did I utter the following fateful words?

"You know," I stated, "I'm going to go back home and raise the money for a bronze statue of Gregorio to put beside Hemingway's in the Central Square of the fishing village of Cojimar where the movie *The Old Man and the Sea* was filmed, and Gregorio lived and Hemingway fished from his beloved boat the *Pilar*. The boat of which Gregorio, in turn, would become captain. Did it get done? Did I raise any money? No! and No! The holes in my colander had grown too big to contain my desires it seems.

But, here I sit in Kabul, having just left the barely, if at all, functioning zoo with an equally ridiculous idea! Or, was it so damn ridiculous to want to help rebuild the zoo where my spiritual friend Marjan once resided, and from where he fought the Taliban so bravely, at least within my story? No, it was not. But to talk about it without some serious forethought was indeed malicious and harmful. It would appear the holes in my colander have grown ever larger over time.

Had I progressed enough in my sobriety and recovery to assume such a mantel of responsibility? Well, it is finally Sunday, and the celebration of the EID holiday, a three-day celebration. Ramadan would be officially ended at dusk tonight. I had absolutely nothing to do or see because every venue was closed. Shut tight tonight. Ah! A fine, warm day of reading quietly in the courtyard, smoking a cigar, and sipping the finest water flavored with Wyler's three calorie packets of fruit powder. Club Med does not get much better. Sandals? Maybe, but not likely. Certainly no burqas here.

Reading, smoking, drinking (Wyler's) and a nap. No kites today. Surprising. I surely thought that was a great way to get through the day, but just not in the city, and certainly not from some dusty, litter-strewn alley near our compound.

No, the hotel boys told me, everyone did not try to stay home (wow). They all met at some park, a grassy area by Kabul or wherever they could all have a picnic. Ahmed was unusually excited that day because his rich uncle had rented a car for the three days of celebration and he had selected Ahmed to drive everyone. He was a pretty damn proud young man, as indeed he should be.

I dozed off later that afternoon. The window was open and the fan was on 'high.' Even at that, though, it was barely sucking in all those late afternoon breezes which lingered in the shade of my porch. Just barely at that. Fortunately, you already know my story about the sheets and towels and bathroom. Yadda, yadda, yadda, as my favorite Seinfeld friend, Elaine Benes, would say.

When I heard a very sharp metallic sound tapping at my window. I looked up and saw an undistinguishable shadow moving beyond my closed and dancing curtains. "Are you in there, Robert?" a voice asked.

I mean, where else in the fucking hell was I

going to be for Christ's sake!

I suddenly recognized the voice. "Yes, Vincent! It is thou? And it is thee!" I teased in reply.

He loved this type of shit. My ex 'never best' Brit expat compound mate. But, much to my surprise, Vincent was soon to be my new very best Kiwi expat compound mate. But, let's not get ahead of ourselves. Ah!

"Come on in, Vincent."

"Are you awake?" he inquired.

Entering is some half-sliding, almost ice-skate-falling, pirouette form that sent the rug sailing and the fan cover falling. It was actually quite amusing in a Dick Van Dyke or Cosmo Kramer type of way. I didn't make any such illusions though, because he wouldn't have known who they were anyway. It was much the opposite of what I once did in Ireland, and then had spent the next two hours watching their beloved Mr. Bean re-runs.

"Hellooo Newman! Or Vincent" I said. "What's up?"

As he prepared to answer, securely ensconced in my desk chair having brushed my clothes onto the floor, his left hand searched the desktop for whatever. However, his right hand was much more determined and focused as it pulled at the door of the mini bar beneath my desk.

"Not much," he said, while his wandering hands sheepishly attempted the magician's primary distraction — the key to their audience control and befuddlement. No, not sleight of hand, but misdirection! "Oh, just thought it would be a grand (not good or great mind you) night for the two of us to visit the "club," he offered. "Maybe watch some football and have a pint with my mates!"

The ever-searching right hand was extended well into the fridge, curious as to what it would find.

"No, Vincent," I said, attempting to relieve his curiosity. "There are no beers in the mini fridge. Just my Wyler's punch."

Dejected, he withdrew his hand, slammed the door shut, and sat up in the chair, immediately blocking the cool breeze from the fan in the process.

"All the better," he said with great glee. "That's why we need to go to the club. We can get cold pints there."

"Get dressed and get out of that damn mini bed, and let's be well on our way before the other blokes drink it all!"

I got dressed, trusting he was not watching my much younger and tanned torso. Just in case, I yanked my wanker once to give it weight. Not weight as if the 1 billionth consumer had said it. It's lovely now, but the *Witches of Eastwick* only blinked three times. Why? I don't know. She smiled, turned to her hubby, grabbed his arm affectionately, and lovingly said, "But dear, length does not matter!"

Yeah, sure, and in what West Coast 60's era drive-in movie theatre was she born? It sure as shit did matter, or we wouldn't have spent very secretive moments of physio-sexual experimentation with the linemen who followed us into battle each Friday night lights at Kiggin Bowl, USA.

Ya adoring and loving late night TV bitch who seeks to sell pills and do great harm to us 60 plus something's who watch your damn show as we are 'winding down' to the lower quarter of our desktop bottles of love. But surely it's not a 'sex' enhancer. Ya, malicious man-hating and husband-baiting bitch, what about what my father told us on a camping trip? "Never go Sunday night swimming nude with your dates in the chilly Lewis River! You'll only regret it on Monday when she goes seeking a new boyfriend who did not go nude swimming with you that fateful night."

Think the Seinfeld and George C. 'shrinkage' episode. Fortified by these and other thoughts, I set out with my new 'leg bopping', Kiwi, Vincent, to whatever the night, and his drunkenness, might hold. Just like two high school genie's off to pick up their 'Sally' or 'Nancy' for a 'Friday night' of no lights at the local drive-in theater.

Off we pranced. Down the dark alley. Together, but most certainly, not 'hand in hand.' Off, against all warnings of danger from local police or Taliban. It didn't really matter, for as I glanced at Vincent beside me in one size checked shorts and a smaller size checked shirt, I knew it was only a stray 'fashionista gendarme' we really feared. (Think

Cocoon or *Oz*)

But, two blocks later, after we checked our imaginary guns and knives at the bunker entrance door to the Univac compound, *10 and behold*, I realized I was the one who had really committed the fashion *faux pas*! For, after surrendering our passports for compound ID's, we stepped inside and '10 and behold' again, my jaw dropped in complete amazement for there before us was a room full of Kiwi/Aussie/Brit beer chugging lads all 'abuzz' about a certain football game on the 'telly.'

They were all dressed like their beloved Vincent. Not one like me. Fashionable in the style of a photo journalist garbed with the best that Exoficio, Columbia, REI and Eddie Bauer had to offer. No, not one single Indiana Jones wannabe.

My self-consciousness soon dissipated when I heard a near unison cheer, "Vinny, Ya got some quid with you for a change tonight? Or, just another new bloke with some Rupees?"

Oh Oh! Been there before! Been there many times before both as a Vinny, and as myself! It will not surprise any of you to find out how the ribald festivities ended, or should I say, started for another 'morn.'

Beers were raised; foam foamed over; cheer for one team or another well bellowed, football turned into cricket, just as toasts turned to arm wrestling and, finally, the burgers and chips were served and suddenly no one (guest or staff alike) was a vegetarian or vegan; but, after 2 a.m., everyone went home. Satiated with food and drink only to be further satiated with dreams of the beautiful Indian girls they never fucked, or for that matter, had even touched, or talked to, or talked of.

That is, all except Vinny! As we stumbled back to the security of the Park Palace compound, he was too damn drunk to be satiated on anything but thoughts of another beer.

The last words I heard him utter as I 'poured' him into his 'single-sized bed' were: "Thanks for the quid, Bobbo!"

Back in my room, I opened my damned noisy Velcro wallet to find one hell of a lot more damage done than a quid. But, nestled among the tattered and faded Afghan Rupees was a yellow folded 'stick-um' note. I grinned, put it back into the bill pouch part of my wallet, and laughed out loud for the first time since I arrived in Kabul.

"Until next time, Vincent." That was all the note said! Sorry Vincent, I'm sure there will be another 'next time' somewhere, but not with me. I am leaving this 'hell hole' with photos, memories, and purloined government coalition documents 'in hand,' and tomorrow.

I am quite sure we will meet again somewhere if only in my words at some cocktail or art house party somewhere, or maybe you will be so honored as to be enshrined in the secretive and revealing conversations of the 'Class of 45.'

Farewell to My Burqa

I returned to my room after a long day and an even longer, dusty convoy from who knows where. I was simply beat. I climbed the stairs to my room, opened the door, and caught myself before I 'crashed' onto my Lilliputian bed. Before me I beheld a small wonder.

My bed was now covered with the most beautiful, white, ironed sheets emblazoned with equally bright blue flowers, the pillowcase matched. Out of respect, I removed my filthy clothes before laying down for a much needed sleep. I slept well, showered, and then went down to dinner.

I had previously learned not to share experiences such as my colorful sheets with my foreign compound mates. Besides, I was now very protective of my 'burqa' and really did not want the others to get flowered sheets for their rooms also. So, I ate a barely edible meal in silence.

It was only a few days before I was to depart Kabul when a very real 'Seinfeld' incident took place. And, yes, it involved my 'burqa.' I was sitting at my desk attempting to open a much anticipated can of Vienna sausages, a very rare and secretive treat during this holy month of Ramadan.

The lid flew off and one 'weenie' bounced from the desk, onto my knee and eventually took one last bounce on the floor before rolling onto a traditional carpet. I looked around; saw no one; then bent over and gently picked the 'weenie' off the carpet and popped it into my mouth, and then I saw it — a shadow.

I hesitantly turned around and saw my 'burqa' waving a reprimanding finger at me. Then she disappeared. Why Seinfelt? Because in one classic episode, George got caught pulling a half-eaten Éclair out of the kitchen garbage bin and taking a bite. His famous response when he was caught was, "but it was above the rim!"

I went to the reception desk for the final time early one morning. Took photos of the staff and myself, and exchanged e-mail addresses and hugs. We had become very close. So close in fact, that I was invited to spend the last day of Ramadan (EID) with some of them and their families in a park by the nearly abandoned zoo I'd visited a week earlier.

I also wondered what my 'burqa' did to celebrate EID.

On the day of my departure, when I approached the checkout desk to pay my bill, I was handed an envelope. I opened it. Feeling all eyes upon me, near breathless, and hearing not a sound except the careful tearing of paper, which is almost just as noisy as the 'not so careful' tearing of paper, I found a letter inside.

It had been translated into English from the native Dari, or maybe Pashtun, language. Here is what the letter said:

"Dear Mr. Bob. You are very nice person. I did not know you before. I do not know any more people from America country. Your money helped my family very much in Ramadan time. All the people here like you very much. You are different and do not leave a mess of bottles by your room door for me to clean. The others are very loud and dirty. Come back. We want you and that you like birds and animals."

It contained no salutation. But, I was soon told it was from my burqa! I was now departing for a very long and grueling trip, and I felt that everything was right in my life. I had made a difference. At least, hopefully, to at least one very special person. I only hoped that my burqa would not change shoe colors before I returned to this wonderful place and its peoples in the near future.

Knowing very well that we always say and think we will indeed return again. Only time and a war will tell.

Gone to India

Exiting Afghanistan was easy, but quite tedious due to their special security issues, and after tearful waves and goodbyes to the compound staff, I was on my way to the Kabul International airport dazed and confused. Once inside the airport, I snapped a few photos of the coalition Helios circling overhead with the majestic mountains in the background, albeit absent any snow. But, no Chinooks! Good for all of us. Today, no damn Chinooks were needed for the coalition troops. Unfortunately, they were certainly needed for us that last day in Vietnam while departing Da Nang under yet another rocket attack. 'In coming' it was always called, and surely not 'yet another,' for all those who would not open their eyes after this attack, or if they were lucky enough to do so, it would only be while holding a compress bandage and pouring sulfa powder onto a sucking chest wound. Those damn rockets might close all our eyes eventually.

"Two Red Bull's please," I said for the first time in my life.

I had just cleared the last security booth and was going to head down the escalator to Gate 2 when I saw the Red Bull kiosk. Never had one, as I said before. I was not really tired, just more relaxed, but I really wanted one.

You know who I am by now, so I really believe I not only wanted a Red Bull, but had to have one to discover what all my young friends claimed was better than coffee. Coffee? Never had that either. My 'eye opener' was a shot of Vodka or rum or whatever was left over, but hopefully not red wine, and readily available, and at room temperature. "Red Bull and Vodka!" they all boasted. Vodka? Now that would be the real difficulty for complete fulfillment as the kids readily claimed. But then, it was morning. Maybe it would work without booze.

While descending the escalator in Kabul to departing Gate 2, I watched in amazement something I hadn't seen before on my excursion into Afghanistan. It was surprising indeed since I'd seen it so many times before in the US on TV, in magazines, and even at the VA hospital once. But not yet on my Afghan trip. Two men in traditional garb kneeling on prayer rugs at the foot of the escalator and bowing (with hands folded towards an empty cement wall) which was surely not to the East of them.

"I thought they only prayed towards the East," I said to a veiled lady beside me. She pointed and said, "They have to kneel facing that way because the Kingfisher Bar faces to the East!"

A short time later, we all filed through exit Gate 2 and walked towards the shuttle bus to the plane. Just as I approached the stairs, I adjusted my briefcase strap and proceeded to grab the handrail when two arms grabbed me from behind. Two hands gripped my arms and another my briefcase and near lifted me up the stairs and into the awaiting bus. Startled, but feeling safe because there were so many others around me, I let the mysterious hands guide me up and onto the last remaining unoccupied seat.

I sat unceremoniously as my briefcase was

placed on my lap, and I finally looked up to see who had been my guardian angels. I was speechless when I saw the two very dignified, tall, bearded, young men who had just a half-hour earlier been praying on their prayer rugs at the bottom of the Gate C escalator.

They stood facing me, bowed, closed their hands together as if in prayer, smiled, and turned to stand at the back of the bus. I never saw them again, and really didn't have to. I would never forget them or their selfless, cross-cultural gesture to assist me and compensate for my weary, broken, and ill-functioning legs.

****

The only way I could ever describe my safe redelivery to India is like being invited to the Prom by the prettiest girl in the class.

With Afghanistan and false but necessary relationships now behind me, I arrived back in Delhi, or would it be correct to say 'arrived back in, left from or back to?' What difference did it really make? Nothing just seemed to go 'to and/or from' on this damn trip anyway. Shit! Had it ever? On any of the hundreds of trips behind me…down the too numerous and readily mistaken 'forks in the roads' which I'd seemed to misjudge in the past and just set out on 'blindly'?

How does one follow up a great day? Why, with another fabulous day of course? A trip to the river that runs by the lodge, across a small creek with very slippery rocks where I fell in — much to nine-year-old Ranya and four-year-old spider boy's delight; followed by a bus trip to the eco-center where we washed an elephant and fed another; to a typical Indian gas station, I am told, where everyone screams with delight as the attendants and driver rock the bus "back and forth" to make sure there is not even 1 ml of gas unaccounted for; to the station bathroom where Ranya announced to me, and the world, that this was the first Indian bathroom she had ever attended alone and without Mom, or even Grandma! Well, then, don't really know how to respond to that one, so it was on to a very exciting and special Jeep wildlife safari with a driver and naturalist and then back to the lodge for a folkloric dance and a Red Bull.

I did not come to India to take photos of those less fortunate than myself. Nor do I believe when I get home, these pictures will make me happier about myself! India is not the underbelly of anything except possibly China! Ditto's with me today, so all is very well indeed.

Rode Ladle, the 32-year-old elephant, going strong towards 132 years of age! As I cruise along some nearly deserted India road, deserted in the sense that there are no more than 1,000 cycles per kilometer, I realize what it is I would love to be 'career wise:' a successful art/movie illustrator. Bar none! But I never will be. I just don't have the talent! So, give up seeing this pleasure? No, I'll just continue being a writer, and possibly just put more animation into my stories.

Wella! Remember the Jim Croce song, *Don't Mess Around with Jim*? Well, I learned a similar warning with the Indian's Tipping scale! **Oh boys or girls, wait until you hear the one about the phantom India tax collector! Or the Indian 'designer' napkin camera case which guarantees your camera will be left behind at least once after a day's meal.

Almost lost it today while the driver rode around in circles for at least one hour seeking the fucking phantom roadside tax collector. My sympathy, however, was not for myself or the other passengers; it was for the professional Indian driver who was profuse in his apologies.

Maybe he should prepare a 'Roads to Nowhere' photo book!

My own life is so fragmented and disjointed that I no longer have the confidence to, even precariously, enter into the mind and/or body of some unsuspecting passerby to see whether they are happy? Bored? Sad?

In many ways, the much heralded vegetarian Indian diet is no more healthy than that of our inner city ghetto dwellers, and I believe we both show it in our youth — and my friend, it cannot be blamed on McDonalds.

Are windows on the inside or outside of a house? Or, for that matter, on which side of the door is the door knob? Just some important considerations which befell me.

Just passed an accident scene wherein a couple hundred spectators (from stopped motor and pedal cycles, cars, buses, and trucks) were gathered around one old turbaned man sitting in the dust. Just holding his ankle and smiling. Apparently, the attention was much better than the pain hurt, and apparently there would be an Indian motor rickshaw riding lawyer there shortly to conduct a 'Pain/Pleasure' roadside examination for a few Rupees.

Pretty much the same as on any highway anywhere in the world when a group of roadside gawkers become hawkers of some other prey's pain and misfortune.

Uncle Buck meets Uncle Bob

I really despise my physical appearance and am afraid I will need to do something anorexic about it — 'really scared!'

Just what in the hell are they all thinking as they squat in their 'Kafkas' beside each kilometer of road our bus passes? The only difference I see is that some of them squat with their hands on their heads ala Vietnamese.

We finally found the tax collector. He forgot to put the 'no tax stop' Sunday sign out before he fell asleep watching the All India/Pakistan Cup match. More important than the 'ashes' they all declare, like we did so many hundreds of years before with our rousing 'Down with the Queen!' OK!! OK!! A possible $100 USD fine for no tax stamp. Seems an excellent trade-off for one hour of wasted petrol in a country much like my own which is dependent on the black tears of Arabic joy.

How can a city look so energetic one minute and completely exhausted less that 1 kilometer further on? Traffic? Dusty sunset? Broken traffic light? Massive construction? Holiday construction shut down? Just as soon as I experienced tossing a coin in the all-holy river Ganges.

Want great six-pack abs? Very simple! Ride a South Asian elephant at least one hour per day! Not only will they become immediately defined, but much larger than those of your friends in the USA due to the metric conversion.

Older Indian (Delhi) women are beautiful, much like the two, wrinkled, red leather chairs I inherited from my parents are.

Pretty touching. Mona gave me a beautiful silver and pearl good luck charm she'd inherited from her grandmother when she turned 13. Red velvet box and all.

How in the hell am I supposed to wear this on my 41-year-old, Vietnam, dog tag chain. I guess I'll have to figure it out because she emphasized that for me to wear such in her absence was very important.

She took me to the Banana Leaf.

News report today, 10/1/2009: thousands died in Indonesian tsunami/earthquake. *Who really gives a shit as long as they don't know one of the dead?*

****

In terminal C, watched an ass pass by that was so huge I wondered who was walking who? Or, much like we say, is the tail wagging the dog?

I then bought an Egyptian excavation kit for my dear friend in India, Ranya. I remembered one day while on safari we'd talked about both of us wanting to travel to Egypt to see the pyramids and the Sphinx. It felt good to share that want. It felt good buying the gift and thinking of her.

I saw an incredibly beautiful Asian flight attendant just pass by. No veils. No burqas! I want to be buried with a 'short stack' of such beautiful things!

As I sit here waiting to board my plane for the nearly final leg home, I'm reminded of something that J. G. Ballard wrote in his book, *The Drowned World*, "Loathsome brute, he commented, then pulled from his pocket a huge rhinestone necklace, still encrusted with algae, and held it out to Beatrice."

I have no idea why that thought popped into my head.

Back in the USA (Chicago)

As I landed in Chicago, I immediately wanted to go back to the Red Bull Kabul time before I let my Chicago customs experience sour me!

Too late.

Just happened.

I'm soured.

After a very eerie 20+-hour flight back to India and the USA (Chicago), I approached immigration. Eerie? Why? Because due to the Air India pilot's strike which was starting that morning, I was the only person in the plane's otherwise empty 24-seat business/Executive section.

Moving on now!

"Where have you been?" asked the young Hispanic customs agent.

"India and Afghanistan," I replied. Then, without another word of conversation, he uttered a very hateful, "They're all just the Taliban's prostitutes. Move on." Stamp. Stamp.

Oh shit! I knew what was sure to happen next from all my illegal trips to Cuba over the last 20 years. Got my bags and was immediately flagged over to the right and asked what illegal items I was carrying.

"Nothing," I said. "At least I don't think so!"

Then, harshly, "Open your bags!" I did and they roughly searched and searched and only came up with a prayer rug my friend Mona had given me prior to departing. "Not for prayer necessarily," she said. "Just a rug for memories."

I repacked the bags without the 'non-prayer' rug or, a humi-sealed, small package of dirt that we took from under the foot of an elephant we saw standing by the road some time before. Mona collected it because it was supposed to be sacred.

Everything is very energized here at O'Hare. Everyone is talking about the 10/2/09 Olympic site vote. Hope they win. No better 'pitch' team than Barack and Michelle.

A group of young girls just passed by in their blue and florescent flight/ramp suits. Each proudly carried a small torpedo shaped vacuum much like the *Bay Watch* babes carried their inflatables, red, skimpy-suited, and into the ocean — or for the more literate out there, remember Graham Greene's classic book *Our Man in Havana* and the atomic vacuum that caused all the trouble?

****

Walking through the door to my house, I suddenly realized that I'm home now. Really home. In Vancouver, WA. Happy, relieved, tired, and mostly so damn glad to be freed of this damn near empty pen.

Final Thoughts regarding my wondrous trip

I did not need to take the perilous, IED strewn, wreckage littered 'road to Kandahar' after all. Kandahar was a destination for younger, better trained, albeit less experienced men such as I. I would only have been in their way!

I learned one thing about Kandahar! It is only frightening if you are afraid of being afraid.

Bob's Kiddie Stories

Baxter the Bear Who Lived
<u>Behind the Water Fall</u>

Baxter, a small brown bear cub, waited impatiently in his cave-like home behind the waterfall. He remembered what his mother had told him before she had left those so many days ago. "Baxter! Do not leave the cave until I return!" she'd ordered.

Baxter spent most of his time lying on his back and looking up at the ceiling of the cave while he listened to the splashing of the water rolling off the falls. His stomach often grumbled and he constantly shivered, especially at night when he was very cold, alone, and scared.

The wet spray from the waterfall kept Baxter's baby cub fur constantly wet. But he always felt a certain warmth when he thought about his mother and the sunny days, wild berries, and honey made by the many buzzing bees which his mother told him were just outside their cave. After listening to such wonderful stories, Baxter would yawn and roll over on his bed of twigs, fir boughs, and ferns and go to sleep.

But with his mother gone, he could not sleep — not without the bedtime stories his mom would tell him. Oh, how he missed his mother, he sighed by way of a partial little bear growl.

The next morning, he was suddenly awakened by the sound of pebbles falling. He laid still, faking sleep while he peeked out of one eye to see what was making this curious sound.

Then he saw a striped shirt and tennis shoes appear at the entrance of his cave. It was little Tommy from the old log cabin by the pond at the base of the water fall.

Tommy had brought Baxter some left over pizza from the old, rusty refrigerator in the cabin. Tommy tried to bring Baxter food every day. At least something he thought a little bear might like.

He knew that Baxter had nothing to eat now that his mother was gone. After warm smiles of recognition and trust, they always sat on the floor of the cave. Just looking at each other, the little boy, the equally little bear just chewing and smiling while they enjoyed the meal, each other's company, and their friendship.

Both of them realized that neither of them had anyone to provide the necessities they would need. Tommy's father had left to go on one of his frequent hunting trips, and Baxter's mother had not yet returned from what Baxter thought was a trip down the mountain to look for food.

After his last visit, Tommy remembered that Baxter was always cold. Even though Tommy only wore a striped t-shirt, he knew he could always start a fire in the fireplace of the cabin to keep warm.

However, Baxter did not know how to start a fire. Nor did he know how to gather and chop wood. The thought of Baxter, cold at night, worried

Tommy. *But, what can I do about it?* he thought.

So, early the next day, before the sun started to warm the rocks at the front of the cave, he visited Baxter. He carried an old wool shirt, a blanket, some white sweat socks and, from under his bed, the hat he got at Disneyland a long time ago. Until Tommy remembered it, it had lain there forgotten and covered in dust.

Tommy actually thought Baxter smiled when he saw him enter the cave with all the gifts. He coaxed Baxter into sitting down on his furry rump as he struggled, but he finally got the shirt onto Baxter. The sweat socks were another matter altogether, though. Tommy had to cut the toes off the socks so Baxter's long toe nails would fit through. The old red blanket was for Baxter at night.

For some reason, the Disneyland hat greatly amused Baxter because he immediately began chewing on it. The hat also brought back many good memories for Tommy.

Tommy and Baxter both grappled with the hat which ended in an old fashioned tug of war. Baxter won and just kept chewing on the hat while smiling at Tommy and drooling out the sides of his mouth. Tommy wondered why Baxter was acting like he was. When Tommy thought of the Disneyland trip, now long ago, he remembered how he'd gotten sick from all the caramel corn he'd eaten.

Surely, it must have been the smell of the old caramel corn on the hat that attracted Baxter,

Tommy thought. Then his memory became clearer as he watched Baxter chewing the brim of the hat. He recalled how he had always rubbed the brim of the hat with his caramel corn-stained fingers when putting it on his head.

While walking down the hill to the cabin, Tommy thought of another thing about Disneyland. The parade with all the people dressed like animals. There was even one little girl in the parade that the kids all shouted to as Goldilocks. And, she marched holding hands with three bears who all looked like Baxter.

Tommy continued down the hill towards home knowing that Baxter would now be warm and sleep well tonight.

Time passed slowly these days. Tommy continued to do his chores in his father's absence and Baxter began to venture out of the cave and climb down to the pond by the cabin. It seemed to Tommy that Baxter was always splashing in the water as if to take a bath.

Maybe he was trying to give Tommy a hint. Telling him to take a bath also, Tommy wondered. No, that wasn't it, Tommy decided. Because Baxter only splashed his paws in the water. Not his whole body.

Little did Tommy know that Baxter was just performing one of the rights of bearhood. Baxter was merely trying, in vain, to catch a fish for Tommy and his dinner.

Tommy had seen television shows of bears doing the same thing as Baxter. But those bears were always very large with equally large claws. And, they always splashed in rivers, not a little pond under a waterfall.

Tommy didn't know that Baxter's instincts were telling him that when the weather became sunny and warm, it would be time to hunt for berries and catch fish, like the other bears did. His mother told him that he needed to be full because the cold weather would come and he would no longer be able to hunt for food.

One day, Tommy looked out the kitchen window and saw Baxter frolicking near the edge of the pond. In his teeth he has a bright, silver-colored fish. Baxter was shaking his head, spraying water left and right until the fish no longer moved. He then dropped it to the ground and looked around at Tommy who was now standing on the cabin porch, smiling and clapping his hands as Baxter brought the fish to him and dropped it on the porch steps.

Another time, while waiting at the cabin for Baxter to return from 'somewhere', Tommy thought about going to the store to buy some 'people food' for himself. Baxter returned shortly, his face the color of dark huckleberries. He saw Tommy, grinned, and let out a satisfied growl.

Tommy made a decision. Now that Baxter seemed to be eating bear food and no longer hungry, he would take his bike and ride to the store for food for himself. Feeling in his pocket, he realized that his thin Roy Rogers wallet only contained one wrinkled dollar bill. Not nearly enough money for food until his father returned from hunting, but Tommy couldn't wait any longer.

He got on his trusty but somewhat rusted bike, and headed down the dirt path to the store. The store really was just a small country market. But, a market with many things he knew Baxter and he liked. Especially candy and pizza.

Tommy put the kick stand down and parked his bike outside the store. The coins from his dad's 'secret jar' jingled with every step as he walked into the store. Tommy suddenly felt guilty about taking money from his father, but what else could he do? He was very hungry and only had the one dollar in his wallet.

Tommy grabbed a shopping basket and began his shopping, all the while feeling very guilty as the coins clinked and clanked with every step he took.

He continued to shop. He'd put many food items in his basket when he stopped suddenly and bent over so as not to be seen. Not quick enough however, he thought as he listened to the people whispering and looking directly at him.

He crouched down further, putting the basket on the floor, and listened intently to what the people were saying — about him…and his father. He crawled to the end of the aisle where he could hear better, and hopefully not be seen.

His eyes opened wide and he gasped when he heard his father's name mentioned — and his name also. "Did you hear about Fred Blair?" one said to the others. "Little Tommy's father. He was arrested again for poaching bears out of season and was sent to jail for three months. Then he could never afford the fine." They all agreed.

Then another person spoke, "He got caught when he tried to sell the hide to some campers in the park." Tommy became nervous because no one had mentioned his name again. Or, if he would be all right without his dad for so long.

Tommy didn't feel very sorry for his dad because he only seemed to care about his son when he needed someone to chop wood, clean the house, and do other yard chores. And Tommy's dad had never even said 'thank you' nor rewarded Tommy for his efforts. Nor had he ever read a story to him at bedtime. Just a hard, drunken slap up against the side of the head if Tommy didn't perform the chores correctly.

The sound of the pilfered coins subsided as Tommy got to his feet again and peered over the top shelf to see who was speaking about his father. He continued shopping until the coins and even the one dollar he had disappeared and turned into two large bags of groceries.

Affixing the bags to his handle bars and basket, Tommy peddled back up the trail and into the woods that surrounded the cabin.

One evening much later that summer, and while he was doing the dishes, Tommy looked out the window and saw something moving in the shadows. He had no idea what it was crawling around the cabin because it disappeared into the shadows too quickly.

He never had visitors, Tommy realized. His curiosity soon changed to fear as his eyes strained to see more movement in the shadows. He turned off the kitchen light and cracked open the screen door to the back porch, silently that is except for one rusty creak!

He opened the door wider and stepped slowly out onto the porch hoping for a better look at what it was that was making the sounds. Much to his surprise, it was only Baxter.

He was no longer wearing the old plaid shirt, socks, or chewing on the Disneyland hat as he crawled slowly around the corner of the cabin.

Tommy's eyes followed him as he entered the field of wild flowers nearby and continued into the darkness of the forest, the same forest that was not so scary in the daylight, but now seemed foreboding and very scary, the same forest that surrounded the cabin, pond, waterfall, and field of flowers, the very same forest he rode through on his way to the store.

Tommy did not call out to Baxter, but just watched him in confused silence as Baxter finally faded out of sight and back into the shadows of the forest where he'd never been before.

Tommy wasn't certain, but he felt he knew that Baxter was leaving him, the cave, and the waterfall. Most likely, he would not be returning.

Tommy picked up the two fish Baxter had left on the cabin porch and went in to finish the dishes. That evening and many others to follow, Tommy's thoughts were of Baxter and he wondered where he was and where he was going.

But one thing was for sure, he would never see Baxter, the once roly poly, brown bear cub again. Nor would he ever go back to the cave or retrieve fish from the back porch steps. Things had changed forever!

The evenings were getting chilly now, so after one more, of many, peeks out the window, Tommy went into the other room and lit a fire. He sat on the old red leather couch and watched the fire glow while pulling a blanket up to his chin. He felt so very much alone.

Tommy awakened just once when the fire was turning to embers and the shadows danced on the living room walls. Making all of his dad's animal 'trophies' hanging on the wall seem to come alive. Then, as he tried to go back to sleep, he realized that, yes, most likely his father had shot a bear, and it just might have been Baxter's mother. Maybe that was why she hadn't returned.

Tommy then fell back to sleep on the couch until he awakened at first light. He crawled up the hill to the cave with a leftover sandwich. As he peered into the empty cave, he realized that Baxter would not come back.

Life without Baxter continued uneventfully until the leaves started falling from the trees, the coin jar under his dad's bed was near empty, and it was almost time for school to begin again. He knew he now had to be brave, and become a boy again. Just like Baxter had become a bear.

Tommy dressed for the first day of school, got on his bike and set off peddling down the dirt path towards the little school house. Then he smiled as he thought about how happy he really was. How lucky that the hide of Baxter's mom was not hanging on the wall of the cabin.

The End

Benny and the crows

Benny was a small squirrel who lived in the ivy hanging from the large white house that overlooked the lake. He lived alone and liked it better that way. He was alone but never lonely. He had too much to do to be lonely.

The snow had melted and the trees started to bloom as they always did this time of year. But it was the warmth of the 'new' sun that coaxed Benny from his 'hideout' home. He was still plump because his supply of nuts and berries had lasted him through the winter.

Then, one day while peering from the safety of the ivy, he saw them. The crows! The always cackling and cawing crows who made his job of collecting nuts and berries much more difficult. Every time Benny climbed a tree or searched the lawn for food, they followed him. They constantly watched his every move when he searched for places to bury his food.

But today it was sunny which made life a little easier. He could now see the crow's shadows in advance of their arrival. For, as they approached from far overhead, they flew in front of the sun and Benny saw the shadows of the crows on the lawn.

Life, it seemed, was back to normal as another season for harvesting had begun. But, this year things would be very different, thought Benny. He had a new and secret way in which to hide the nuts and berries he had collected. Yes, he grinned, it will be a lot of fun fooling the crows.

Benny would collect twigs and leaves along with the nuts and fill his cheeks until they felt like bursting. He would then scurry across the lawn and bury the twigs while keeping the nuts in his puffy cheeks. The crows were occupied digging in the spots where they thought Benny had buried the nuts as Benny quietly snuck into his ivy hideaway.

The crows continued digging in the very same places that Benny had buried the twigs. Benny laughed a high-pitched squirrel laugh as he twitched his bushy tail at the crows from within the small hole in the ivy.

Benny slept well most nights while nestled safely in the ivy listening to the sound of the crickets just beginning their work for the night. Benny did not really know if the crows ever slept. They disappeared towards the lake each night and returned like clockwork the next morning. As Benny awoke, he wondered why it was that the crows always wanted to eat the same food he did. *Maybe they can't find any bird food*, he thought to himself.

Life in the ivy and throughout the large yard was a constant wonder to Benny. One such wonder was whenever the old, gray-haired lady who lived in the big house came to the back porch; Benny could always hear the screen door squeak as she opened it. She then always sat in the same green chair and tossed a mixture of nuts and seeds on the lawn.

The crows always came down first to steal the food, but the old lady always scared them away. It seemed to work because they flew away to who knows where, and didn't return for the rest of the day.

The Blue Jays were a completely different matter. Yes, they were much noisier than the crows, but the old lady didn't shoo them away like the crows. She obviously thought they were pretty. But, as cute as Benny? He surely hoped not.

Benny approached the food as he always did and the lady threw more seeds on the lawn in front of him. Even though he knew the lady well by now, he still approached her with caution. The old lady never shooed him away because Benny knew she liked squirrels as well as the Blue Jays, for that matter, much better than crows.

Then, many weeks later, when the sun began to set earlier and the chill was again in the air, the old lady was joined on the porch by an old gray-haired man. They sat side by side on the porch. The lady throwing out the seeds while painting a picture as the old man read his newspaper and smoked his pipe. For some reason, the old man never threw out any seeds.

Then, one day the old man came out onto the porch alone. He sat down as always and started to feed seeds to Benny as the woman had done so often before. He was not as good at it as she was and oftentimes threw the seeds too far. In fact, so far that the crows could get to them before Benny. The old man continued to come out alone for the rest of the summer. Sadly, Benny never saw the old lady again.

Then, one Fall evening before the dew was on the lawn, Benny realized that he had enough seeds, berries, and nuts to last through another winter. He felt bored and started to wander to other places in the large yard that he hadn't seen before, but he always returned to his ivy home before dark.

Just before going to sleep, Benny noticed the light from the house shinning on a spot of grass just outside his home. He wandered out to look at it more closely, and for the first time, he saw the old man sitting alone at a table in the window.

Across from him there was an empty chair. No one ever sat in it as far as Benny could tell. The old man just continued to eat his dinner slowly and sometimes looked out the window, but he never saw Benny sitting on his haunches, his long tail curled beneath him as he watched from the shadows on the lawn below.

The light went out while Benny still sat in the shadow looking up at the window. The old man left the dining room and went to another room, the one with the smoke coming out of the roof. The old man turned on the light in this room and disappeared from sight.

Soon Benny went to bed still wondering why the old man was alone, and where the old lady had gone.

Fall turned to winter and the sound of the geese flying in formation overhead reminded Benny that the first snow would be coming soon. One cold, snowy evening Benny noticed that the lights in the house were not shining anymore. Curious, he wondered why?

One thing that Benny immediately noticed was that not even the old man sat in his chair for dinner. Now there were two empty chairs at the table and no light whatsoever.

On closer inspection, Benny realized the house was empty. No smoke came out of the roof any longer and no one came to the back porch anymore.

Then, some days later, Benny heard laughter and many different people sounds coming from inside the house. He squatted in his regular place on the lawn and peered in the window just as all the lights seemed to come on at once. Benny, afraid to be discovered, crawled deeper into the shadow.

Soon after this occurrence, Benny realized that there were now many different people at the table and all of the chairs were once again full.

Benny soon realized that there were new people living in the house and none of them were the old man or woman. Maybe they had moved to another house, Benny thought. Wherever they'd gone, Benny was sure that they were together. Reading and throwing seeds and nuts to some other squirrels.

Benny didn't mind. He was happy for them, but would miss them. Then he fell asleep that night to the sound of the crickets and selfishly wondered if the new people in the house would like the crows better than him.

The End

The Cricket Who Wore Tennis Shoes

The cricket did what he did every night before he went to work. He sat on the ledge of the old white house and watched through the window as the people inside turned on the television.

He always hoped they would be watching the TV show where the people on it played some type of game where they hit and chased a small white ball. But, most of all, he liked the bright white shoes they all wore. "If only?" he surmised.

"But not tonight," he chirped to himself. Instead, they were watching something with people with big hats and guns who rode horses that made a lot of dust. "Maybe tomorrow," he whispered.

He hopped from the window sill onto a branch of an old tree and then hopped once more to the ground. It was now time to go to work. The cricket liked his work, as did all the other crickets. Their sounds seemed to make everyone happy. Especially on a warm summer night.

By constantly rubbing their hind legs together, they made a melodious chirping sound. Benny the squirrel who lived in the ivy especially liked the cricket sounds. In fact, one day Benny told the cricket that the sound seemed like music and helped him get to sleep.

Benny was the cricket's good friend. He always brought the cricket some nuts to eat not knowing what crickets actually ate. They seemed so small and thin, they must not eat much, he thought.

Because of his friendship with Benny, he was afraid to tell him a great secret he had been hiding for a long time. Benny had always been a good friend to the little cricket, he never teased him about being so small, and he'd never thought his words sounded crazy. So, on one warm summer evening, he decided to approach Benny with his idea.

He nervously sat by the door to Benny's house in the ivy just as Benny peeked out the hole to see who was scampering about outside his home. He saw the cricket and said "hello."

The cricket said he would start work soon so Benny could go to sleep, but he needed to chat with him first.

The cricket then asked Benny if he had ever stood on the window ledge of the people's house and watched the television. He knew Benny hadn't done so, but he felt he had to ask. Benny's tail twitched back and forth in its usual excited manner as he answered, saying, "No! I never have, but I've always wanted to."

So, the cricket asked him to watch with him the next evening knowing that Benny would have to be up past his regular bedtime to do so.

"Sure," replied Benny. "We'll do that together tomorrow."

The cricket smiled, and then went to work doing what crickets do. Very soon after, Benny fell asleep inside the ivy.

The sun arose bright the next day as the cricket was safely sleeping in some long grass by an old wooden fence in the yard. Benny was turning over frequently trying to get some more sleep before beginning his day of nut and berry gathering chores. Neither, though, forgot their conversation of the night before.

That evening, they met on the grass below the window of the people's house. Benny was a lot better climber than the cricket, but the cricket showed him a short cut through the tree's branches to the window's ledge. There they sat together and waited for the people to turn on the television. The cricket said he hoped the show with people wearing white shoes would soon be on.

The cricket suddenly started furiously rubbing his feet together and smiled at Benny as he made a very high chirping sound. The cricket was very excited as he pointed towards the television. He saw that Benny was also looking, but in no way as interested or excited as he was.

Yes, the people chased a small white ball wearing white shoes just as the cricket had said they would, but Benny thought it was nothing special. Benny then thought a moment. The scene on the TV was very similar to what the people in the house did with their dogs: throw a ball across the lawn for the dog to bring it back, only to be thrown again.

When the television finally went dark, the cricket told Benny he had to leave for work just as

Benny needed to go to sleep. They would talk more about the cricket's secret tomorrow, now that Benny had seen the television show with the white shoes.

Late the next afternoon, the cricket came to talk with Benny. It was much earlier than usual, but he didn't think Benny would mind. Besides, the cricket needed some daylight to explain the secret wish he was eager to share with someone.

The two of them sat just outside Benny's ivy house as the cricket pointed to the sky. There, up in the sky, was a long wire high above the ground. It hung between two large poles. Benny knew it well because it was one of the places he climbed to escape the dogs.

But what did the cricket find interesting about the wire, he wondered. After much pointing and chirping, Benny finally understood the cricket's wish and why he could not find it alone. The cricket could not climb the pole or walk on the wire, Benny concluded.

What was the secret? High up on the wire hung many pairs of tennis shoes. Sometimes the neighborhood kids threw them up so they hung from the wire. Neither Benny nor the cricket knew why they did this, but the cricket was sure happy they did.

For up on the wire hung one especially bright white pair of tennis shoes. The cricket knew them well because he'd been looking at them for many weeks and just dreaming. Dreaming of having them and wearing them when he went to work at night. He would be the only cricket with white tennis shoes — shoes just like the people wore on the television.

Benny had a plan, but the cricket already knew what it was. Benny would climb the tall pole, crawl across the wire to where the shoes hung. He would then chew through the lace which held the shoes onto the wire. The shoes would surely drop to the ground below so the cricket could have them.

They parted with the cricket going to work and Benny to his much needed sleep. But not before they agreed to meet the next evening just before dark.

The sun rose bright in the sky the next morning as Benny returned to his regular food gathering chores and the cricket slept restlessly at the bottom of a large bush. His dreams continued throughout the day, never wavering from the thought of his white tennis shoes.

The sun started to set. Benny was done with his daily chores and the cricket was sitting safety under the bush. They met at Benny's door while it was still light and before the other crickets were awake.

They crossed the lawn and hopped down a long slope until they were standing under the wire from which the shoes hung. The wire was so high, thought the cricket. He hoped Benny wouldn't fall and get hurt.

The cricket watched closely as Benny disappeared from sight and then reappeared halfway up the pole. Benny only looked down once before he proceeded to cross on the wire to the shoes. The cricket became worried that Benny might pick the wrong shoes. But, he had nothing to worry about as Benny made his final steps across the wire and stopped right at the white pair of shoes.

The cricket became so excited when Benny started chewing on the laces that he didn't realize he was rubbing his rear legs together and making a very excited cricket sound. When he realized what he was doing, he immediately stopped. He didn't want to awaken all the other crickets and let them know his secret. They would surely think him a fool. Also, it was forbidden to start work so early.

The cricket watched Benny chew through the shoe laces and then chirped with glee when they dropped to the ground in front of him. His dream had come true. He watched to make sure Benny got down the pole safely, and then chirped a very quiet "thank you."

Nothing mattered to the cricket anymore. Not his work or watching the people's television. He chirped another thank you, and Benny told him it was a really good chirp. Benny scurried away to his home in the ivy, leaving the cricket alone with his shoes. The cricket then put on the shoes. They fit perfectly.

He did an awkward hop step up onto the lawn to a place near Benny's house where he usually worked. Work did not seem so boring now, he thought. And, the shoes were even bright white at night.

As the other crickets started their chirping, he started rubbing his legs together. But, no chirping sounds came out. He had promised Benny his best cricket sounds that night. He rubbed harder. And faster. Still the cricket sound did not return.

As tears came to his eyes, Benny came out of the ivy, wondering why the cricket had made no cricket sounds. He looked at the sad little cricket, so sad with his feet so large and white. They both understood that the cricket was having a very serious problem. They both admitted that wearing the shoes would keep the cricket from making his wonderful night time chirping sounds.

The cricket hadn't thought of this before. And now he knelt on the lawn very sad, but knowing what had to be done. He carefully took off the shoes and set them beside him as Benny approached closer.

Benny grabbed the laces in his mouth and held tightly as he dragged them across the lawn to the place where they fell under the wire. When he returned, the cricket seemed embarrassed, but somewhat better. He had stopped crying, and whispered to Benny. "I guess crickets are not supposed to wear white tennis shoes. Only the people on the television should wear them."

He realized that he was supposed to be a cricket not a person. Benny listened and agreed, telling the cricket that by tomorrow things will be better, and then he returned to his ivy home to sleep.

The cricket waited for Benny to disappear into his house before he hopped close to the ivy doorway, really closer than he had ever been before and he started the most beautiful and special chirping serenade just for Benny to hear.

The End

Jimmy the Burro Whose Feet Were Too Big

Jimmy clearly remembered the day he was born. He remembered the straw itching the new soft skin on his stomach. He was only two weeks old now, but he still couldn't stand up like the other burros who lived in a corral at the edge of a high cliff. In fact, his skinny little brown and white legs felt as if they weren't even part of his body.

Each day, all the other burros came to the corner of the corral where Jimmy lay. They all stopped to look at him and made a very loud braying sound to each other. Then they all did the same thing, they all put their right foot forward and placed it next to Jimmy's right hoof. They brayed louder and in unison.

Jimmy felt good receiving all the attention he did, but didn't know why he was getting it. The others eventually all backed away and trotted to their own places in the corral leaving Jimmy still wondering as his mother came close; she bent her long neck and kissed Jimmy on the nose. He then rolled over on his other side where it was easier to eat the straw, flicking his long tail at the flies as he did so.

The days became longer and warmer, but Jimmy still had trouble walking on his own; at least now he could finally stand up like the other burros. He could stand up and bray and even put his two large front hooves on one of boards in the corral fence. None of the other burros could do this. Nor, did they seem to care.

One day Jimmy finally asked his mother why all the other burros looked at him in such a strange way? Before his mother could answer, Jimmy told her how lonely he was during the day when he was left alone in the corral. All the other burros went down a steep dusty trail with Cowboy Sam carrying a lot of 'people tourists' as the other burros called them. Then Jimmy's mother nestled her nose into his side and started to bray the answer to the question Jimmy had asked.

"Jimmy," she said. "You were born with very large hooves, and Cowboy Sam said it would be too dangerous for you to carry a tourist on your back and go down the steep rocky trail into the canyon. I know you are lonely during the days being in the corral alone. But all the kid tourists come to see you and feed you sugar cubes."

Jimmy knew she was right. The kid tourists were very nice and they all petted him when they stood by the corral. Then she whispered so none of the other burros could hear. "Someday you will be very famous, and all the other burros who have been so mean and laughed a bray to you will be jealous." She continued whispering into his fuzzy and floppy ears. "You will be different," she continued. "But there is more to life than taking the tourists down the trail with Cowboy Sam. You will someday find the burro job that is best for you, and I will be so proud of you." Jimmy lay down on his side and smiled.

Mother was right, though. Tonight I'm going to have some good and exciting burro dreams, he thought to himself. He ate some straw and blinked his eyes in slumber. His long eyelashes blocked the rays of the warm, setting sun and he went right to sleep.

One day, Cowboy Bob was in the corral spreading new hay for the donkeys to eat when they returned from the canyon. Jimmy watched Cowboy Bob as he worked, and then he suddenly stopped and walked over to the corral gate.

Standing outside the corral was a man, a woman, and a little boy. The boy was leaning on two sticks and seemed to have trouble standing without the help of the man and the woman. Jimmy saw Cowboy Bob talking to the people. Curious as ever, he trotted over to the gate, his plate-sized hooves stirring up a whirlwind of dust.

He listened while Bob asked the people if they could return in an hour. They said they could. They were staying at the large lodge which was only a short walk away. A short walk for the man and woman maybe, Jimmy thought. But a longer walk for the little boy with the two sticks under his arms.

Cowboy Bob then rubbed Jimmy's wet but warm nose and went out the gate of the corral. He walked slowly towards the little red barn, creating his own whirlwind of dust as his old cowboy boots dragged through the dried dirt. The boots seemed as tired and old as Cowboy Bob.

Cowboy Bob was in the barn for what seemed like a long time before Jimmy saw him come out carrying many things that looked heavy. As Cowboy Bob approached the corral, Jimmy immediately recognized what it was he was carrying. He had seen all the other Burros wear them when they took tourists into the canyon.

Cowboy Bob opened the gate and put the many 'burro things' down by Jimmy. Jimmy sniffed and brayed in recognition. There was a bridle; an old, red, Indian blanket; reins; a saddle; and an old, sweat-stained cowboy hat. Jimmy had never seen Cowboy Bob wear the hat before.

Cowboy Bob petted Jimmy as he gently placed the blanket on his back. Pretty soon Jimmy was wearing all of the real 'burro things' but could not figure out how the hat would fit over his ears. Jimmy became very excited at being a real burro at last. He stood in wonderment, and watched Cowboy Bob closely as he placed the old, stained cowboy hat on the fence post by the gate.

Cowboy Bob then did something that made Jimmy very curious. He was holding a square white fence board with writing on it and making pounding sounds as he hung the sign on the coral fence. For only a brief moment, Jimmy saw what was written on the board.

It said, "Come see Jimmy the Burro with the world's largest burro feet. Bring a dollar and you can even ride Jimmy and wear the cowboy hat. You can be a real cowboy." Jimmy thought he knew what the sign said, and just as he was thinking about it, the little boy with the wooden sticks returned to the burro coral with the man and woman tourist.

Cowboy Bob opened the corral gate, helped the boy walk to Jimmy, and placed the old cowboy hat on the boy's head. Jimmy came closer to the boy, nervous but very excited. Cowboy Bob gently lifted the little boy onto the saddle and placed the wooden sticks next to the gate.

Jimmy didn't know how he knew, but he knew exactly what to do. He walked slowly around the corral as he felt the boy tighten his tug on the reins. Around and around they went as Jimmy's smile got bigger and the boy's voice increased to laughter. Around and around they went.

When Cowboy Bob signaled Jimmy to stop and come over to the gate, the boy pleaded, "One more time, Dad. One more time, Mom."

"Maybe tomorrow," they answered. "Remember, your legs will be very tired from riding Jimmy so long."

Cowboy Bob grabbed the wooden sticks and helped the boy to the ground. Jimmy watched, knowing the little boy had a hard time walking just like he had a difficult time trotting. Jimmy then came to the conclusion that both had a problem with their feet. Jimmy's were too large and the boy's were too small. He no longer felt alone.

The people left with the boy, and Cowboy Bob led Jimmy into the barn and took off the saddle and all of the other burro equipment. Then he led Jimmy back to the corral just as the other burros were returning from their job of taking the tourists down into the canyon.

Jimmy was awakened each day to the gleeful sounds of the excited children. They were peering into the corral and calling out, "Jimmy where are you? Jimmy, we want to be a cowboy." Each day the line seemed to be longer. Still, the children tourists waited patiently. Some wearing cowboy clothes, but all clutching a dollar bill in their hands while the parent tourists stood by, watching and sharing their children's excitement at being a cowboy, or a cowgirl.

As the weather turned cold and the skies gray, the tourists who wanted the trail rides became less and less. Then the rains came and made the trail impossible for tours. Still, Jimmy's line of tourist children got longer and longer.

One day a large truck pulled up next to the corral, the other burros brayed as if understanding the reason for the truck and lined up at the corral gate.

As the other burros got onto the truck, Cowboy Bob pulled Jimmy and his mother aside and kept them in the corral. The next day, Cowboy Bob led Jimmy and his mother into the barn, laid down some nice fresh hay, and gave them a new and warmer home.

Later that day, Jimmy saw Cowboy Bob talking with some people from the lodge. He heard them say, "Even though the trail rides are over for the year, the tourists would still be coming to the lodge."

The man from the lodge who was doing the talking, pointed to Jimmy and his mother and said, "Cowboy Bob, you and Jimmy are part of our family. You are very important to us. We need you, Jimmy, and his mother to stay with us through the cold months. The tourist children will need you also."

Jimmy looked closely at the lodge people, Cowboy Bob, and his mother. He now knew why he and his mother were not in the truck with the other burros 'going south' for the winter.

Cowboy Bob led Jimmy and his mother into their new home in the barn. He petted them and gave each of them some carrots before he left closing the barn door behind him.

Jimmy brayed loudly and smiled so wide his large, white, and square teeth protruded in front of his lips. Jimmy's mother also smiled. They both understood that Jimmy was now a very important 'cowboy' burro; he was no longer just a burro with two very large awkward feet.

She would always love him no matter what size his feet. After all, he was the only baby burro she had.

The End

Sidney: The Frog Who Would Not Hop!

Way across Farmer Brown's field, almost half a mile from the old, red, and sagging barn, was a small pond where the lily pads and flowers covered the water like an emerald-green carpet. The lily pads were just large enough to hold two frogs: usually a mother and one of her frog babies as they watched the other frogs swim, chase flies, and play their other silly frog games.

Nothing seemed to bother the frogs. The farmer never came down to the pond anymore; his grandkids had grown too big to fish. The frogs missed the kids because it was fun to watch them fish.

There were not many fish anymore either to keep the water clean, but the newts, salamanders, dragon flies, as well as the water-skippers still lived there — living side-by-side with the frog family.

The only possible danger to the frog family came from their friend Bob. Bob was the old raccoon who came down to the pond late each night to fish for crawdads in the small stream which flowed into the pond. Bob wandered happily, splashing and slapping his big bushy tail on every rock he passed as if in warning to the frogs who were safcty hidden in their little frog homes under the pond's bank, or those who were trying to sleep in the hollow of the walnut tree which lay half-submerged in the water.

Bob usually visited around midnight. Splashing as he washed what it was he'd caught for his late night supper. He always seemed to eat late, they thought. The frogs only stopped their serenade for a moment as they heard Bob arrive. *A bothersome noise*, the frogs thought.

Not at all as pretty as the songs of the bluejays that awakened them much too early each morning, sometimes even before sunrise. Thoughts such as these always made Bob tired. The croaking didn't really bother Bob as much as it distracted him.

So many croaks in a row, Bob thought. Croak, croak, croak.

The frogs didn't know it, but Bob actually enjoyed the sound of their croaking. They did know that the croaking sounds made it harder for the crawdads to hear him splashing as he came down the stream.

The frogs, however, knew their croaking kept them safe and actually scared Bob off and away from their pond homes. But none in the frog community had every read whether or not raccoons liked to eat frogs.

Life at the pond continued as always with the old frogs leaving for 'frog heaven', and young ones being born nearly every day it seemed.

The farmer continued to plow the fields around the pond. Even though now, with his eyesight failing, he came less and less to the shore where the long grass grew.

The sky began to turn a softer shade of gray as it always did this time of year as the crickets and ants kept busy preparing for the first signs of winter.

Each winter, the pond froze regular as clockwork. The frogs, burrowed safety beneath the banks of the pond, as they prepared to hibernate and wait for the long winter months to pass. The only sound that occasionally disturbed their slumber was the cracking of the ice in the stream as Bob searched for one last meal.

As the frogs huddled together warm, safe, and sleepy that winter, they listened to Bob one last time as he grunted and slipped on the icy pond. They all felt sorry for him. He always seemed to be alone. He was constantly hungry.

And, he never seemed to sleep. No matter how much fur he seemed to have, they all thought he must be cold on winter night like this. But as the nights grew colder and the days much shorter, they forgot about Bob and drifted into a long winter's sleep.

Then in spring, as the frogs began to awaken, the days became longer and the ice on the pond began to melt. The ducks returned flapping their wings on their way to some mysterious place in the south.

The bees once again started to buzz above the flowers by the edge of the pond and the farmer's tractor could once again be heard in the distance.

Winter had passed, and the frogs anxiously anticipated the warm days of swimming and frolicking in the pond. But something interrupted the frog community that spring. Something that would change their lives forever.

Early in May, a new baby frog arrived in their community. She was different. Try as they might, none of the other frogs new exactly why. They named her Sidney.

It had only been a month since Sidney arrived, but already she was the 'talk of the pond!' None of the other frogs could take their eyes off her as she swam back and forth from the shore to the lily pads.

She seemed so confident and adventuresome. So unafraid. And, oh so indescribably different. But, try as they might, none of the other frogs really knew why. They all agreed. Yes, she was somehow different from any frog they'd ever seen.

Like the day she lost her tail and was no longer a tadpole. She was not sad like the other frogs who lost their tails or the people from the farm for that matter, who worried when their kids lost their first tooth.

The frogs knew about first teeth because they had always listened to the farmer and his red-haired grandsons as they stopped the tractor by the pond to check out the fishing.

"Something about putting a tooth under the pillow," the farmer had said to the boys. *How silly,* the frogs thought. *Can you imagine trying to put our tadpole tails under our pillow of twigs and leaves?* Human people were very silly. Especially those who rode the tractor around the pond.

Life continued quite normally at the pond until a short time later when something very strange happened. Even little Sidney didn't know what it was. But suddenly all the other frogs realized how Sidney was different from all the other frogs. One day they all stopped what they were doing and starred as Sidney went down to the pond for a swim.

Even the water-skippers seemed to watch in amazement. For Sidney didn't hop to the water's edge. She stood up on her hind legs (although somewhat shaky) and walked into the water.

And then, as if to make matters more strange, she dived into the water. Yes, dived in. Not head first like the rest of them, but much more graceful, like the two ducks who landed on the pond each evening just before dark.

This had never happened before. Even the oldest and wisest of the frogs had never heard of a frog who didn't hop... and most certainly, never a frog who walked. Only *people* like the farmer walked, and sometimes Bob, but never a frog, and certainly not Sidney.

All that spring and summer the frogs watched as Sidney walked everywhere she went. Almost as if showing off, she walked to the edge of the pond, over rocks, logs, and finally to a stump near where the tall grass grew.

Oftentimes she would climb up on the stump, stand up, stretch on her hind legs, and just look around. Looking out towards the farmer's fields, and then looking back at them, her confused but amazed audience. She knew she was looking at things the other frogs could never see.

Through early summer, the other frogs, old and young alike, would gather around the base of the stump and ask her questions. Ask her what she saw. Could she see the farmer's house? What was in the fields around the pond? Their supply of questions seemed endless. Their curiosity increased daily.

But, in all this commotion, one other thing seemed very unusual for Sidney's young and untrained senses. The weather seemed to be getting hotter. She had no experience in matters such as this, but she sensed something as she stood upon the stump.

She was still a young oddity, but she listened to the other frogs below her, and they constantly croaked about how the weather seemed so different.

Sidney grinned as she stretched herself on the stump and let the warm wind blow across her little belly. She had many other important things to concentrate on these days that she felt were more important than the weather. What one may ask?

Why the many incessant questions from all the frogs circled around the stump.

There were just so many answers for all of their questions. They did not understand, but she was only able to answer questions about what she could see. And sometimes, in a joking manner, she just answered to fool them.

As June settled into July, the frog community usually found Sidney at her post atop the stump. What they didn't know was that Sidney, even on hind legs, and perched atop the stump, could not see much more than they.

For poor Sidney, no matter how much she stretched, could see no farther than the grass the farmer had mowed. He no longer mowed close to the pond, so the grass was quite tall. Still, she spent a good part of each day standing on the stump answering all the other frogs' questions.

There was, however, one thing Sidney could see and it frightened her very much. It was how small the pond was becoming. There was now a very strange mud appearing where water used to be.

As she stretched and looked back over the shore of the pond, she thought she could actually see the pond shrinking. A strange, cracked, brown mud now stretched from the pond to the submerged walnut tree where Bob once fished.

She hadn't thought of Bob since last winter. Where was he? What was he doing?

As the days passed more slowly and the pond got smaller, Sidney became more worried. She desperately wanted to warn the others, but would they believe her? After all, she was only a little frog who had never even been to the far side of the pond by herself.

And so she continued to worry — about everything it seemed. The mud got larger and the pond grew smaller. Then, once again, like that day weeks before, when she felt the hot breeze on her stomach, she shuddered in fear. Fear of something she didn't know. What about the pond, flowers, lilies, and old Bob? Something was wrong. She was just a small frog, but she knew something was very wrong.

Still, she climbed up on the stump each day and felt the wind getting hotter, while the other frogs huddled below her in the shade of the old rotten stump.

Their bellies were cooled by the damp grass beneath them. They didn't sense the danger because from where they squatted, the shadow of the old rotten stump protected them from the wind.

Besides, from where they squatted, they could only see as far as the edge of the pond, and not any farther. Eventually, they became tired of hopping to hear Sidney, and stayed all day long in their rapidly shrinking mud houses.

As the days continued to get hotter and the wind blew dryer, dust began to fall on the ever-shrinking emerald green pond. By the first of August, when the farmer no longer came to the fields, the frogs became concerned. It was now becoming a long hop to the cool waters of the pond. Many, in fact, thought the journey of hopping to the pond was too much work, so they stayed in their mud houses.

Even Bob seemed different and did not come to the creek every night as usual. His favorite stream no longer rushed over the rocks and sunken log, but now ran underneath them. The noise of the cool brook disappeared, and the crawdads along with it.

Finally, one day in the middle of August, Bob disappeared. Sydney was the only one to see him go. One evening, just before sunset, she saw Bob crawling up the diminishing creek. Tail no longer wagging, as he headed to who knows where? Maybe the farmer's red barn?

They all missed Bob as the days continued to grow hotter and longer. Without Bob, was there any reason to keep on croaking every night? Now that Bob was gone, was there any danger?

They all felt guilty. Bob, they all agreed never really posed any danger. They just liked to croak when the moon came out. And now, having the pond to themselves, it didn't seem the same.

The lilies soon dried up, and the mud that used to be fun to hop across, was now hard and cracked. Even the many bugs had left or been blown away by the increasingly strong warm winds.

The frogs became more frightened by the changes each day, and no longer felt like leaving their houses and making the long trek to the decreasing pond. They now realized one of Sidney's secrets. The pond was drying up, and they had no place to go.

They felt they had to escape, but they could never hop across the farmer's field that surrounded their shrinking pond. As they thought of Bob's departure, they realized that not even the strongest of them could hop to the red barn.

Besides, who of them even knew if there was another pond by the pond where Sidney said Bob went. They all felt better as Sidney stepped down from the stump and told them there was another pond over there. One that held crawdaddies, lily pads, and flowers as theirs used to only a few months ago. Sidney thought of Bob and hoped that he had found another pond.

The other frogs gathered around and asked the same question, "But what about our pond?" Suddenly Sidney had an idea. An idea that might save them all. Maybe, just maybe, she could get up on the stump and stand a little bit taller. Stretch a little bit farther. Just maybe.

She thought, *maybe I will do it tomorrow before it gets too hot. Just before I croak to the others gathered around the stump.* Then, maybe she would be able to see the pond that was supposed to be by the red barn. The very pond that Bob had waddled towards.

Tomorrow arrived much too soon. Hotter than ever. *The wind is blowing even stronger than yesterday,* Sidney thought as she headed for the stump. All the other frogs stayed in their cool mud houses.

As Sidney got on the stump and stretched her legs to the fullest, she immediately noticed something was very different. She could actually see past the barn. But she became alarmed that the wind was getting hotter and the grass around the stump was getting yellow.

The barn! Something was very strange about the barn. It was redder than usual. Redder than the sun in fact. And there were red and black clouds coming out the windows and door. Red and black like the bellies of the newts who used to live under the log at the far side of the pond. Red and black like the clouds that were now reflected in the pond. It suddenly got darker. *It's too early for sunset,* Sidney thought.

Over the tops of the yellow grass that surrounded the stump, the heat came. She cried privately. Not because she was afraid, but rather she did not know what to do to stop it. Then there was lightening that she hadn't heard for some years — not since the time when it struck the old walnut tree and it fell into the pond only to become Bob's home.

The other frogs, hearing Sidney's alarming croaks, came out of their mud houses and stood in amazement. Then they saw what she had seen. The dangerous clouds Sidney had warned them about Then they saw something she had not told the about. Something that was even more frightening than the red and black clouds from the barn. They saw Bob — running before the clouds. He quickly disappeared into the diminishing pond, and then quickly surfaced only to smile and lick the water from his whiskers. Immediately, they felt relieved and happy. For a brief moment, they even forgot about their worries.

Surely Bob would not let the black and red clouds hurt them. He swam to the half submerged limb of the walnut tree that he liked best and wondered what Sidney would do next

Suddenly, it came to her as she stood high on the stump and all the other frogs' questions came to her. She remembered the old walnut shells and pieces of bark Bob had dislodged in his search for food. Walnut shells from the old tree had been turned over in search of food, and even the shells of the crawdads.

As the fire approached, one by one the little-legged fire brigade hopped to the edge of the pond with their makeshift buckets. Dipping them into the pond and returning as fast as they could towards their mud houses. Fearlessly, they approached the flames only to stop their hopping to find their spill buckets empty. They tried to hop slower so as not to spill the precious water, but nothing seemed to work.

The pond water still spilled from their buckets with each hop; it spilled onto the caked mud and cracks that surrounded the pond. They all watched in amazement as the black and red clouds came even closer.

Then they saw her. On the stump just looking as smoke curled around her. Then she hopped down, stood on her hind legs, and went to the water's edge. Her little chest heaved in exhaustion as she grabbed walnut shell after shell. She walked slowly at first.

Then she ran filling each shell with water and pouring it on one of the frog houses, only to return seconds later to do it all again. Not a drop was spilled because she walked and didn't have to hop. All the other frogs cheered. And then the cheering stopped. They all looked up and saw the red and black clouds were slowly disappearing.

The clouds disappeared and Sidney looked at the water dripping from the tiny houses she had soaked with water. The houses had been saved.

That night, after washing themselves and cleaning their tiny houses, the frogs rested. Then they approached Sidney; they didn't know what to say. Sidney just smiled at them and knew things would never be the same again. She thought of the stump, the red barn, the farmer, and all the things that had once mattered. Certainly, there would be other things that mattered just as much?

Then, they all heard him! Splashing around by his favorite log only the splashing seemed different. It was much louder. Like the way the creek used to sound as it went over the rocks. Sidney left the others and ran to the edge of the pond. There, she saw Bob! He had a lily pad on his head as he stood looking up at the sky from which the rain was falling in torrents.

The End

The Littlest Poinsettia

He had always remembered being nearly the same size as the other poinsettias in the jungle around him. Now, almost all the others seemed so much taller and had many more leaves. Maybe it was the shade he lived in below the palm fronds high above. No matter the reason, he was determined to be tall and ready for Christmas which was arriving much too soon.

Yes indeed, his leaves were a much brighter scarlet color than all the rest, but that might not be such a good thing. The farmers might notice him first and pull him from the ground and drop him into the 'discard' truck. But then he thought about it; surely the other poinsettias would somehow save him, and then he would be able to sit proudly in someone's window, on a table, or best of all, below the green Christmas tree awaiting Santa's arrival. Knowing how important this was for the littlest poinsettia, all the other plants tried to gather around the 'little one' to hide him from the farm pickers.

Hiding the little tike was not that easy due to his brilliant leaves which remained much brighter than all the others. Still, they bent their trunks, gathering around the little one like some nurturing mother protecting her newborn.

The sound of the truck in the next field was now much louder, and its big rubber tires kicked up a cloud of dust as it came closer and closer to the new field of poinsettias.

The workers in the truck sang some foreign song as they picked up their shovels and stepped down into the new field. Pretty soon, the workers came within only two rows from the little poinsettia. He shivered with fear beneath the darker leaves of the poinsettias protecting him. He felt like crying as his fear grew. There was just nothing he and the others could do to change anything. It was now left up to sheer luck.

He let out a muffled sigh as he was cut from the ground and gently placed in the truck with all the other plants. Yes, he realized. He was one of them. His leaves relaxed and drooped as did all the others as they were safely on the truck. The last thing he remembered before they went to sleep that night was that they were all together.

All the next day, the truck bumped and bounced down the rutted gravel road. The truck engine made a deep, low, growling noise as it struggled towards its destination. All the poinsettias except for the littlest one knew their final destination. They had heard the workers talking about it.

"Be ready for a warm and kindly home for Christmas," they told the little one.

They would be placed in special cardboard containers to keep them warm and safe during the long airplane flight to the 'cold country' where Christmas was celebrated. But now, some of the oldest poinsettias told him to get ready to get on a people plane.

Soon the air in the plane became colder and all the poinsettias huddled together once more. Then they pulled their maroon leaves over their exposed trunks and got ready for a good, but noisy, sleep.

The great big plane stopped with a whining sound and all the doors were automatically opened. For some reason, there were no people on this plane. The boxes were then immediately shuffled around and lifted from the plane to an awaiting truck with flowers painted all over it. But there were no painted poinsettias; these came only once a year and were not important enough to be painted on a truck.

The plants were all wrapped with a beautiful red and shiny paper. Something like a hood was put on them to keep them warm. They were once again loaded onto a smaller truck which drove silently away. It made no noise because the road was covered with fresh snow.

Shortly after the truck came to a stop, the back door was opened. The first thing all the poinsettias saw were the excited faces of a young boy and girl. The funny looking dog with them just barked and waited for one of the kids to throw him another snowball.

The kids pointed and gestured towards the 'littlest' poinsettia. The truck driver carefully took the plant down from the truck and handed it to the little girl. "Make sure it gets inside the warm house," he said. He knew that the cold outside would kill the poinsettia if it was left unattended by the kids.

The funny looking dog immediately stopped what he was doing and ran towards the little girl with the poinsettia. Then the children went into the house after first stopping on the porch to stamp the snow off their boots. The funny looking dog was told to stay outside.

Once inside the house, the children placed the littlest poinsettia under a large green tree and close to the fireplace. Too close it turned out. It was placed right in the spot the dog had always called his own. That night the mother and father joined the children in decorating the tree. Always carefully stepping around the little poinsettia.

When it became so cold outside that the dog was let in, with tail wagging he rushed to the very place where the 'littlest' poinsettia sat. The dog would have nothing to do with this intruder and began wagging his tail furiously against it until the little plant fell on its side. The mother stood it upright, but a few minutes later, the dog's tail knocked it over again.

Dizzy from the falls and too hot from the fire, the little plant wobbled side to side as it waited for another sniff and push from the funny looking dog with a very wet and cold nose.

The mother realized what the dog was doing and picked the little poinsettia up and very carefully carried it to a window lit by colored lights and heaped with new snow. The dog barked once and followed the woman. The little poinsettia was clearly confused and waited for another attack by the funny looking dog.

The littlest poinsettia was finally home. The dog was far below him, and the children soon tired of hanging sparkling things on the tree and went outside again to build a snowman.

The little plant turned its leaves towards another small poinsettia on the window sill. "Hello," he said to the little red poinsettia sitting next to him. "Please tell me about your own long journey to the sill here."

The End

Timmy the Turtle Who Went to School

I have never hurt anyone, Timmy thought as he swam as fast as he could to a little sand island in the middle of the pond. He felt safe there. His home was under a big rock on the island.

His little fins, like feet, paddled as fast as they could, which was not very fast. Only 'turtle' fast. He continued his swim to safety as the many rocks and pebbles, thrown by the farmer's boys, bounced off his shell. The boys always threw pebbles at him when they walked by the pond to go fishing in the river nearby. The same river that flooded the pond and the little frog's houses during a long rain storm. Timmy had never seen the river, but had heard his friends, the otter and the beaver, talk about it often. Besides, if the boys were going to the river, then Timmy did not want to go there anyway.

Timmy made it to the island and the safety of the cave under the big black rock just as he heard a loud scream. It was a little girl with golden hair from the farm waving a stick at the boys to keep them from throwing pebbles at Timmy. She was dressed in a pink dress and shoes. Timmy had never seen so much of this pink color before. Nearly everything growing in and around the pond was green.

The boys laughed at the little girl and began a game of sword fighting. They had their bamboo fishing poles while she had only one small tree branch to defend herself. The boys soon became bored playing the pirate game and continued to follow the dirt path towards the river and away from the quiet pond where Timmy and his many animal friends lived mostly undisturbed.

This occasional intrusion by the boys continued off and on until the end of summer. After summer, Timmy would not have to worry about the boys throwing pebbles at him, or whether the little girl would be there to make them stop.

Late one day, after the boys were chased away by the girl, something very strange happened and Timmy became afraid. The little girl, still wearing her pink shoes, sat on the grass surrounding the pond staring at him. Finally, she took off her shoes and laid them beside her. She then stood up holding her dress high and carrying a very pink bag on her shoulder, she walked carefully into the pond.

She waded out very slowly, the water not being very deep, towards the sandy island. Each step brought her closer to Timmy. He tried hiding under the rock that was his home and listened to the little girl's splashing as she approached.

Timmy peeked out from under the rock from time to time, hoping the little girl would not see him hiding. She continued her approach, however, until she finally set one foot in the sand of the island.

The girl was his friend. Still he tried to hide deeper under the rock. Timmy continued listening as the girl knelt into the sand on both knees. Then she peeked into his hiding spot and spotted him. He peeked back with wonderment in his eyes.

Timmy suddenly became very frightened as the girl reached under the rock and pulled on his hard, green shell until she brought him out from under the rock and into the bright sunlight. He was more afraid of the two boys learning this trick than he was from the girl's intrusion. All the pond animals immediately stopped what they were doing as they watched Timmy be placed in a bag on the girl's shoulder. In a flash, they all returned to the safety of their own homes.

Timmy blinked rapidly with his little eyes as the darkness came. She tied the rope of the bag and reentered the water for her return trip to the far shore. Timmy nestled in the soft bottom of the bag and tried to be calm as the bag bounced with the girl's every step.

After what seemed like many bounces, the girl stopped walking and placed the bag on the ground. Thank goodness the bouncing stopped, Timmy thought. Then suddenly it got bright again. Peeking out from the bag, he saw the bright sun. Then he smelled something very familiar. It was the smell from the large animals he often saw walking in the field around the pond.

The animals seemed to walk and walk without getting anywhere. They would often stop, lower their heads, and begin eating the grass. After eating a lot of the grass, the animals looked up and made a loud noise. A second later, he heard a whooshing sound come from under their tails, followed a moment later by the very smell he instantly recognized.

It then became dark again even though the bag was still open. Timmy felt the bag move. It left the ground and was placed under the porch of the small white farm house. Some lettuce leaves where placed in the bag and then it was tied shut. It was dark again.

Timmy knew that lettuce was a very tasty food, but he had only eaten it once before because it was not something that grew near the pond. That time was when a piece of it fell out of one of the boys' sandwiches and into the shallow water that surrounded his island.

Timmy laid at the bottom of the bag only hearing the crunching from his chewing the lettuce while crickets chirped somewhere nearby. He finally closed his eyes and fell asleep feeling comfortable and warm.

He was rudely awakened by the pounding of feet stepping on each porch step. Soon the noise approached his pink bag hideaway. The bag was untied and the girl fed him more of the lettuce. Then, the bag was closed and lifted from the ground and onto the girl's back.

After what seemed like a long timel, Timmy felt a very strong bouncing as the girl walked up some more steps. He then heard the screams and shouts of excitement coming from many children.

The bag was again placed down on a hard table and opened once more. Timmy saw the daylight again and many eyes peeking in at him. "Timmy is here. Timmy is here," he heard them all shout.

The pink bag was opened and Timmy was gently pulled from its safety and placed on a large, hard, wooden table with many other animals. He knew some of them from the pond, but the others he had not seen before. Some were very strange looking, he thought.

Timmy then looked around and saw the large room, heard more noises, and watched the other animals approach him. He was no longer afraid when he saw the little girl and felt her paste something on his back. It was a piece of paper with a number on it. Just like most of the other animals wore.

A bell was rung loudly again by the old lady sitting at a large desk in the front of the room. She rang the bell once more and told all of the children to go to their desks immediately. The children became silent and sat down like the old lady told them to do. Their backs became straight and motionless as they stopped speaking. Then, they picked up a little yellow piece of wood and began writing in a small book.

It looked like fun, Timmy thought. He wished he had one of the little yellow sticks like all the other kids.

The animals on the table just walked around

in circles touching noses with each other. Some even approached Timmy and licked his always cold nose. But, no one wanted to touch noses with the scary animal in the wire cage.

They were all afraid if it, as was Timmy. It had very narrow yellow eyes and made a hissing sound if any of the other animals approached his cage. Timmy sure hoped that the scary animal would not be let out of his cage.

Then, after what seemed like a long time, the kids' voices became excited and loud again. They left their seats and stood around the table listening to the old lady tell them the rules of this game Timmy was part of.

None of the kids made a sound while the old lady spoke. Then they were told to go back to their seats and pick up their little yellow sticks. They opened their books and wrote something. Timmy did not know what they wrote, but it was surely part of the game, so he too paid attention while the old lady spoke.

The old lady called out a number and the some of the kids raised their hands then wrote some number in their little books. Another number was called and some different kids raised their hands and wrote some numbers in their books.

This went on for a short time. When the numbers had all been called and written in their books, the old lady told them again to be silent. They quieted immediately, put down their yellow sticks, and looked nervously around the room.

Then the old lady began to call out some numbers Some of them raised their hands again and started bouncing in their seats, sat on one leg tucked under them, and listened as the numbers were being called out.

Timmy heard some oh no's and awe shucks. Then some yeas and hurrahs, as three of the kids left their desks and approached the table and pointed at their animals. Then the old lady called out three numbers and the kids again became silent.

Timmy watched this game and was very happy that the dangerous animal in the cage did not wear a number. Its number was stuck to his cage and not on him.

One freckle-faced little girl picked up her pet rabbit and lifted it above her head as she called out her number. "Third," the old lady said.

Then, a little boy with a torn shirt and dirt on his hands lifted a Guinea pig above his head and called out his number. The old lady said, "Second." The little boy hugged his pet and took it to his seat with him. He looked very sad and began to cry.

Timmy then felt himself being lifted off the table and held high above the little girl's head. Timmy was now very excited because he could see all the kids at one time, and all around the large room. He liked being held high up. He was always so low to the ground at the pond.

The teacher then said, "First place" as the

little girl walked around the room cheering and holding Timmy as high as she could. All the other kids, and even the old lady, clapped their hands as the little girl and Timmy walked up to the front of the class. Both Timmy and the girl were excited as well when the old lady put a blue ribbon around Timmy's short and wrinkled neck.

The old lady rang the bell again and called out "class dismissed!" It was time for the kids to gather their pets and head for home. School was over for another day. The animals, and even the scary one, were taken by the kids back to their homes in barns and fields that surrounded the farm houses where they all lived.

As all the kids left the school house, Timmy heard one girl say "congratulations" to the little girl who carried Timmy on her back. Timmy was the winner of the contest called 'show and tell!' The girl and her rabbit walked off in another direction, she stopped and turned her head to say good-bye to the little girl and to Timmy.

It was then time for the little girl to take Timmy back to his island in the pond. They both 'bounced' their way back in the pond.

When they arrived, the little girl pulled Timmy carefully from the pink bag, and then looked carefully for the mean boys before she carried Timmy across the pond to his little island. He was laid on the warm sand; he blinked a goodbye to the girl before starting a slow crawl to the large rock. He decided he needed to sleep. It had been a very exciting day for him.

The girl returned to her house while Timmy nestled in the safety of his cave under the rock. Timmy thought she didn't know he had one of the short yellow sticks hidden between his jaws. He wondered if the little girl knew he'd taken it from the bottom of the pink bag.

Timmy's eyes started to close in relaxation from the warmth beneath his belly shell. He really did not know if he was awake or dreaming as he thought, *now that I have the yellow writing stick, all I need is a bell like the old lady who the kids called teacher.*

Sleep easily came over him.

When he awakened to the early morning sunlight, Timmy remembered only one of his many dreams. He only remembered standing on his rock, ringing a bell with the yellow writing stick in his mouth. He then gave all the other pond animal friends a number. He did think it might be difficult to teach his friends the game called 'show and tell'.

But he would try.

How would I ever be able to put the paper with a number on the water skippers backs? he wondered. They were much too small to play this game, and too fast as they crawled back and forth across the pond. He would figure it out, he decided. Then he waded into the pond and told Bob the beaver about the game, and about his long and exciting journey to school.

The End

The Buffalo and the Blogger

Yes, they were a team, a most unremarkable one at that, and they were also friends, vets, companions, and romantics.

One lived within the realm of technology and all that inspired and created, the other, placidly grassed in the lowland plateaus in search of grass with which to grow his *non-technical* fur in preparation for the winter to come.

The blogger, like some medieval court jester, had mastered all the new technologies that his society offered. The buffalo, however, admired him greatly for this deed, but did not know what he was doing. He only heard him talking into some black thing he held to his ear occasionally.

But, the buffalo thought, *I'm more interested in grass than a cell phone.*

He kept on chewing the grass and seeds while the blogger, in the comfort of his basement office, kept searching for what was new.

In fact, he constantly sought the newest in technology, but he always shared it with the buffalo. He didn't seem to have anyone else to share it with. He knew his friend the buffalo would always listen.

Although the buffalo loved the blogger, he felt sorry for him. He had never seen his house, and most likely, the blogger did not know his prairie home either. That's just the way it is. At least with a blogger and a buffalo.

The buffalo always liked it when the blogger came to visit. And he also liked his horse. The same black and white type of horse that his grandfather buffalo had painted on his tee pee when the buffalo was young.

He knew the blogger was a kind man with many curiosities which he would never understand. For, just as the blogger reached the fence enclosing the meadow where the buffalo fed, there was always a loud ringing noise.

And, as always, as in times before, the blogger reached into his saddle bag and retrieved some black object that rang and rang and rang.

The buffalo did not like this noise because it reminded him of the bells on the wagons that crossed his plains so many years ago: the wagons that held the shooters. The same shooters who made his ancestors run and run and run but were never able to escape the sound of the guns.

Personally, of course, the buffalo didn't remember those incidents himself, but he'd heard other older buffalos talk about such. He forgave the blogger knowing he was not one of them, and because he liked the way he treated his horse.

But the buffalo was very concerned for the blogger because of all those special and noisy things he carried with him. He also rode his horse like he knew everything there was to know.

So, why did his friend the blogger ride out each and every day to speak to the buffalo? He always stopped by the fence, tied up his horse, and beckoned the buffalo to approach. However, the buffalo who was not used to being given orders always relinquished because he liked and trusted the blogger man.

"How are you Mr. Buffalo? I know your life is very different from mine, but, can you please tell me how cold the winter will be?"

The buffalo just snorted a frothy breath, clawed the ground with his hoof, and looked at the blogger.

"Thank you, Mr. Buffalo. I can see by the redness of your fur that the winter will be long indeed."

His friend the blogger rode off to wherever it was he'd come from. Now, there were no strange noises to interrupt the Buffalo, noises he would never understand.

He always missed the blogger as soon as he rode away to wherever it was he lived He snorted, bent down to eat some prairie grass, and wondered when, if ever, he would be invited to visit the blogger at his home.

The End

Poetry of Robert Henry Walz

Depression
(an ode to my shrink and
the first poem in my poetry book)

Depression
some have it
some don't and
I do not mean
a shrink
but depression
one of the cruelest
afflictions a god
ever bestowed upon
mankind or at least
part of mankind
the cruel part
I inhabit and can't
share with anyone
for it is truly an
indoor sport and
between the sheets
of an unmade bed
which will never be
made as long as the
occupant remains
depressed
I once read that
depression was a
self infliction of
the weak but

I wonder often
like alcoholism
is it my fault
sure does when I
am depressed
and a trip to
the bathroom to
brush my teeth
is as difficult
as the Marine
Corps boot camp
I endured so
many years ago
when the only
depression
I knew was an
off base weekend
hangover which
I thought was
hell in itself
but I was wrong
terribly wrong
as the first
incoming rounds
hit home and
readily killed
my buddies
but compared
to their
families I had

nothing to be
depressed about
but I soon forgot
about then
and was depressed
now
and a days
accomplishment
is turning off the
porch lights or
bringing in the
papers
and dusk is no
different from
dawn because
the blinds are
drawn tight
and my only
respite is next
weeks meeting
with my shrink
and pretending
for five days
that I am
normal
until the shrink
and I
next speak

<u>Dancing on Broadway</u>

I feel like a monkey
dancing on Broadway
but no one looks at my dancing
— just that I am a monkey!

Ten-Foot Wall

A 10' wall
was in every prison
the Nazis ran
if only
a brutal reminder
of what Adolf
left behind

it was much more
than a wall
as so many Jews
found out
it was the new Reich
where bullets were

no longer wasted
gas was much cheaper
but still
the Jews stood tall
against the black wall
swallowing their passion

and praying
for a freedom
that would not soon come
at least to the wall's
victims
whose blood was now black
against a full moon

The Congo

the Congo
aids
a new name
a republic
was where I once went
to discover myself
alone and quite scared

I flew to Benin
as far as I could go
from there on foot
and by any vehicle
that would take me
was a welcome surprise
It cost me some bottles
sold by the roadside

I was still quite young then
back from two wars
I book deck passage
ended up on the stern
in a hammock with others
who drank, fucked and sang

it was appropriate
and what I sought
until the monkey was caught
and put on a pole

intestines below him
his mouth in a growl
still alive

and hoisted
as some Joan of Arc
to his destination above
deep in the ship's smoke stack
he writhed on a wire
just wanting to die
but his meat would be better
if he was smoked alive

that's what they told me
as they offered a piece
of a once live monkey
still charcoaled
and blackened

Black Dog

we were in Cuba
a long ways from home
looking for senoritas
not the black dog
which we hit
with a rental car

I laughed
and pretended not to care
a puppy it was
like Kennedy at his death
I pretended to Emmy then also
that I did not care

I cried for weeks
and sought to lessen the bounds
not of my conscious
something else
I have not yet found

I will never be happy
because happy means hurt
the dead dog is lucky
he dead under the dirt

No thoughts of worms
or meals missed
only a deep sleep

before he will be missed
I feel the same
most days of the week

the black dog is my friend
each night before bed why?
because he is dead
he is darkness
and cannot hurt me
and I am not light but together
we make — nothing
So now I will sleep.

There is no snow in Cuba
so he will always be black
unlike Christ
he will never come back
his tomb has been selected
by the side of the road

and, no one really knows
since we passed
except the wheels of the car
who will never forget
but I,
unlike the dog
live every day with regret.

The Bird on the Pavement

the bird on the pavement
it was only a bird
as far as I could see
its wing still flapped
with nowhere to go

on a street in New York
as most people watched
not helping at all
as I approached
and cradled it in my hand

squeezing it's life breath
between my fingers
'cause no help was on hand
I did not want it to suffer
alone by itself

so I did a Kevorkian
and snuffed life
by myself
I was sad
but the bird was quite happy
because he was flying
at last

so much for life
on the pavement

hot
with gum stains
and quite harsh
what did it matter

the bird was no longer
there
nor was I

My Wife

my wife
of sorts
was still my wife
as I entered
the bar
and my guys
with whom
I drank
each evening
as she did the
same
but somewhere
else
hardly a marriage
but still some
love remained
but only late at night
when I came home
drunk
and she came home
stoned
and our paths
did meet
in a torrid embrace
which really
meant nothing
the next morning
when I realized

205

that one cannot
unfuck his wife
it seems

<u>Younger Sister</u>

younger sister
having one can be
either good or bad
bad for sure in your
youth when all they
do is ask many questions
and play with your stuff
but later in life
hopefully
they will be good for you
especially after a war
and not ask so many questions
but provide needed answers
to questions you now ask
about life in general
and your foibles
which may have caused others
some pain and hardship
but hopefully they will
forgive you and no longer ask
so many damn questions
that now seem quite
innocent in retrospect
because they mature so much faster
than an older brother
who in age becomes
the younger brother

Hungry Man

sometimes my life seems
as fleeting
as a hungry man
eating his first meal
at McDonalds
after getting out of prison
where he had to eat slow
and protect his food
with an arm above his tray
as all prisoners do
to celebrate
their daily feast
of apple sauce and
mashed potatoes served
with corn
always
and smelled of
some other inmates sex
but not his own
for now out he could proclaim
himself a prison virgin
and eat whenever and
wherever he wanted
to eat
but always
with his left
arm protectively
above his plate

some habits
never die
nor are ever
noticed
at his neighborhood
McDonalds
except by another
ex con as he

Famous?

Someone recently asked me if I wanted to be
famous? My answer:

I already am
genetically speaking
in thought, word and deed
thanks to Mom

I surely know such
and, it is inevitable
Mom taught me this
on her first trip to Vietnam

I hid for a week
just like any proud Marine would.
She found me
as did so many others

circumcision, an act that we encounter
when very young
mothers watched the process
just like they did with the removal of tonsils

it was part of what made them mothers
and, mentors
as which was not certain
with fathers

but, I am much older now
and the only wars I fight are my own.
the circumcision pain still lingers
I thought I heard the doctor whisper to the nurse

it should be the first, and only pain a child has to
endure
I proved the doctor
and nurse
wrong

Maybe it wasn't
a one-time pain
to me, or hundreds, thousands and millions
of others

times have surely changed
I am sober now
not that sobriety is all that matters
to myself or anyone else

but it made me a much older person
I still do not listen to the doctor's orders
nor, do I believe that bedtime stories
can lull a child to sleep during a war

I no longer hate women
but do like them
but,
always remember that

I will always fall in love with a women
as broke as a car that won't start
in a liquor store parking lot
she will get home with her bottle somehow

my sobriety is not fun
I wish it needed me as much as I needed it
like sitting in a wicker chair
in front of a bullet riddled Mexican wall

the wall needs me
to prove that
a massacre did actually exist

sobriety is fleeting and scary
just like the concept of infinity
that I cannot get my hands around
it is much too slippery

but, I surely do not want it to last forever
forever is much too long
and fleeting
like the goose feathers

and bits of green shredded hip boot
on a remote rusty barbed wire fence
a memorial
to the goose that got away

the disgruntled hunter

home by now to his loved ones
who wants to hunt again
and cannot escape his addiction.

Politics Aside

politics aside
is an aside in itself
to disguise what we
really mean by
politics aside
absolutely nothing
as I watch a western
with Jimmy Stewart
who know nothing
about politics aside
but as I watch
he is falling in love
with a lady of course
who loves him back
in a western movie
which has not politics
but a lot of bad men
and good men
and no Indians
but over the horizon
the Indians come
and kill anyone
in sight
including
Jimmy Stewart
and really wish they
could shoot
arrows into all of the

white kids watching
the on television
and keeping count
of the red man
and not the white
hats
while they wore
their coonskin caps

I know what you mean

I know what you mean
I heard as I walked into
the boulder hospital ER
I saw my two patients react
in disappointment to the
doctor who said such
a doctor who knew nothing
about suicide as the kids
and I sure did so I threw
him against the wall and
told him I wanted to see
his wrists knowing full well
security would come soon
when I previously told them
I know what you mean I
meant it and was not proud
to say it but they understood
and felt comforted and told
me so as I finished bandaging
their wrists which were sliced
and we all watched the doctor
try to get off of the floor
but they feared this morning
just after the grades came out
and were posted for all to see
on a board in the hallway of
the college they would soon
have to leave with a promise

unfilled to their parents and
each other
to notify their parents was not
a responsibility of mine just a
volunteer at the hospital and
in life I suppose but to comfort
them was my honor and duty for
I truly knew what they meant
as I looked down at my own wrists
scars glistening from a soured
relationship so many years ago
and the pain still hurts a lot
so I wished them well and to get
out before security came and
they said thanks and that if their
grades would have been better
they would have been able to stay
at the same college and in love
but now

Iliad

it all started
with what I thought
was just a joke
but apparently
my shrink and
my liver doctor at

the VA did not think
it was such for they
corralled me in a room
at the hospital too
ask me to better
explain my comment

but doc
all I meant was that
I would rather die in
Afghanistan than in my
bed at home with a
pistol in my mouth or

as cops say "I ate it"
their retort but you are
not even a soldier anymore
to which I responded
once a Marine
always a Marine

so they suggested
that I go to Ward five
for 72 hours of wellness check
by even more shrinks
as if that would solve any of
my problems but miss my flight

so I bolted from my chair
through the half opened door
only saying to them that
never interrogate a person
in a room in which the door
does not always open inwards

suicidal yes and a recovering
alcoholic surely but not
crazy, for a crazy person
does not go to a war zone
in a Muslim country
especially during Ramadan

where a drink was not going
to be available in the country
but surely crazy to spend the
money on a first class ticket
to Karachi on a flight where
drinks would be free for 21

hours and there was no one
to see me or catch me
instead 72 hours later I was
sneaking into Afghanistan
on a fruit convoy from Peshawar

Pakistan over the Kkyber pass
to an unknown destination
somewhere in Kabul
sober and sweating profusely
which I blamed on the heat and
humidity but not my withdrawal

I arrived weaponless even though
there was no TSA or shoe searches
when I joined the convoy
surrounded by hundreds of
AK-47's destined for who knows where
I said I was Canadian because

everyone likes Canadians
and the Irish but not so the good old
US of A for assholes
scared and forlorn I was
standing at the curb where the
truck dropped me before the

Canadian embassy with bags
smelling of bird shit and
rotten mangoes thinking that

just maybe the 72 hours in
ward five did not sound so bad
Canadian after all was the name
of my favorite whiskey called mist
the bunkered compound guards
sent me across the street
to an international bunkered
compound but not a glass of mist
I ran as fast as I could dragging

my pack and a duffle bag through
the darkened streets with a pack
of dogs howling at my fleeting
movements as I stumbled and
just a few yards from my goal
I would meet the dogs later

a flashlight went on a short
distance away and then the smell
of cigarette smoke that comes from
bunkers in any war as the guards
do anything to stay awake and
alleviate their boredom

after entering through three armed
bunkers giving away gifts from my
rein stash as I stopped for each search
body check and received a sawed-off
12 gage shot gun as a gift from the
compound front desk and I asked

about a permit and was told
you are in Afghanistan buddy
what do you want a slingshot
just return the gun when you
depart of give me $100 and
I will report it stolen and it's

yours for a souvenir because
you will not need it when you
rent a jeep because you also
need to hire a guard and
translator as well as a driver
but it's only 150 dollars a day

I was awakened abruptly by
an incessant tapping on my
window much like the sound
of a key or coin on the glass
but not all that sure I slept
but I sure had a bad dream

which made no sense as I did
not know where I was nor did
I recognize the apparition in a
purple burqa peering in the
window of my claustrophobic
cell-like bedroom container

I looked up once and waved
her away at least I was sure

I waved but she did not go away
back down for more sleep
and hopefully not back to my
sweaty, vomit inducing nightmare

in which I was on a very large
raft of plywood sailing into the
Kabul Harbor under the cover of
night with cages of falcons at
my feet trying to keep dry as
I poled towards shore and an

unlikely and uncertain war of
which I just joined as the burqa
again woke me up with my pack
unopened beside my Lilliputian cradle
my duffle as a pillow the other
not to be found by me at least

at three o'clock in the hot Kabul
night with sounds of helicopters
overhead and not a good sign about
no more nightmares to come to me
in just another foreign war for
which I volunteered without any

skills as were needed so much more
now than in my prior war in S.E. Asia
this time she had the front desk
guy with her and I could actually

see his smiling, youthful and not very
vengeful face peering in my opened

room door but just a crack he later
said to Mister Bob as I would forever
be called while I was in country or
until years later when I ventured
to another foreign shit hole
equally unprepared except for

REI and my (sorry REI) Eddie Bauer
luminescent army style watch which
in retrospect was not the best
watch to wear in a war zone unless
you wanted to be identified as those
who should be in a war zone

Mister Bob time to move to which I
thought to where I just got here
still barely awake he grabbed the
duffle while the burqa grabbed the
much heavier pack and onward we
trundled towards a new room to

where I did not know nor did they
two care as I followed in full
conversation in English nevertheless
to the burqa and her purple crocs
muttering something about how I
knew the creator of the croc who

lived next to me in boulder Colorado
I was sure she would take this snippet
of information home with her to impress
her family but before I could take
another step she opened the door to
my new palatial habitat and half

carried me to my much larger cradle
while the desk clerk watched quite
surprised they left, I closed the blinds
and slept a fitful sleep of boa constrictors
with babies in diapers on their backs
when I awakened I heard the muezzin

call the people to prayers and my call for a shower
delightfully warm with ivory soap and I
dried off with a towel stolen from another
hotel named park palace so forever my new
home would be the park palace to me
now downstairs for dinner and what not

only to be confronted by a table full of
west Africans awaiting dusk to eat for
the day with a red and white KFC bucket
of chicken and napkins on the table oh how
I wanted to make a comment about the
water melon being missing but I did not

and walked by towards the cafeteria
my mistake because when I returned

to my room they intercepted me and
asked me to join them in conversation
which not only turned out to be exciting
but quite informative and my true entre

into an Afghanistan that I never would
have seen on my own and by the end of
the night they had me getting married
to any number of the single ladies
back home in their tribal homelands
quite a compliment really considering

my grizzled looks and seemingly not so
svelte posture and lack of tattoos and
bone ear rings and feathered boa but
what the heck we bonded at the expense
of one of their homeland sisters and
when they said Bob see you 5:00 am

I wondered what they meant then one said
we deliver ballot boxes to Masir-el-Sharif
an old bastion for the Taliban some seven
years ago when or special forces had defeated
them only to shift to Iraq and let them come
back again and try to disrupt the elections

I had read the book Horse Soldiers so was
at least literarily knowledgeable about our
destination in northernmost Afghanistan
a real Taliban site in my second day in country

was unbelievable and a falconry enclave

the chopper departs from the flight line early
so bring your own breakfast and dress warm
we will see you in the lobby and yes bring your
blue handled shot gun we have not extras
sleepless but with no dreams I got up at 4:00
and walked to the courtyard bundled and armed

and hungry and thinking about a shot of vodka
with Clamato and a celery stalk and what could
that hurt anything at least since I was not flying
but my chances for such were about as good as
my flying the Africans to safety after the pilot
was shot and my marrying the chieftain's daughter

so I walked to my room just before dusk with
no rounds expended but hopefully I will see some
ground fire tomorrow just as the fucking shrinks
feared and maybe they were right but I am not
really sure at this point in my journey to where
I still do not know except that falcons and
quite possibly imprisonment brought me here to this
unforgiving land the imprisonment I had prepared
for with the help of my neighbor Jim who tied me
to a chair in my Vancouver back yard and let me
sit exposed for six hours without water in 100
degree
heat so I would know what it would be like to

be a Taliban prisoner and the Taliban did not know
the wily tactics of my prisoner coach Jim who
asked me to masturbate every night so the Taliban
devils could not coerce me with female flesh but
then I shuddered to think about what flesh
was under my purple croc and burqa-wearing maid.

The End

The Crow

The crow
stole
the rose
right
out of
my hand

before
I
gave it
to Noelle
I suppose

I remember
buying it
I think
not
the crow

but
the rose
as
I
look down

I see
petals
black

feathers
so

I really
do not
know
if it
was

the
rose
or
the feather
I gave
to Noelle

Allergic to Sincerity

allergic to sincerity
is the only safe place to be
whether hiding from
neighbors, friends or family
who all want a part of me
and I do not have that many
parts of me left
they have already
picked me clean
almost to the bone
but in reality
I readily gave up my flesh
with kind gestures
and acts of kindness
which were never acknowledged
or ever returned
so here I go into the abyss
of near solitude
a place so dark that
I only care about myself
and now select the others
I want to care about
it might take a while
to still keep the vultures
at bay and hungry
and to finally find
lightness in my cave
of self concern

Two Drunken Men

two drunken men
fell into the Seine one cold night
when the water was almost frozen
when they jumped for the boat
that was no longer there
but was
10 pints ago
when they last saw it
accidental deaths the coroner
called it
not noticing that both
had small incisions on the back
or their heads
and the same crucifixes around
their swollen necks
which meant in France at least
that they had robbed a church
and penance was to be had
at all costs
since the two men were priests
their cassocks bloody
and water logged
and on their way to the eternal kingdom
where wrong would be made right
but not the money left behind

A Fantasy Land

a fantasy land
of liars
is a place I well know
and hid in like others
who denied their strength
to be anything other.

it is a very murky world
where lies build upon lies
until the truth
not be told
as the bible says.

but this land had no
rides or roller coasters
but only those who trusted
no one not even themselves
and continued plotting
their very next move
just hoping they can
keep the dragon
close
and
at bay

<u>My Long Walk</u>

my long walk
to
nowhere
really
started
at
birth
and
shortly
after
when
I
took
my
first
steps
on
a
journey
called
life
but
I
soon
realized
I
could
not
go
backwards
any

more
because
I
had
already
been
there
which
enabled
me
to
forget
the
man
I
brutally
killed
in
a
bar
fight
over
nothing
more
than
a
lying
cheating
wife
who
was
just
like

me
it
seems
and
to
this
day
keeps
me
awake
at
night
sweating
and
guilty

<u>My Wings Fell Off</u>

my wings fell off
for
the
first
time
the
night
before
my
first
wedding
when
my
bride
to
be
said
she
was
a
lesbian
and
the
ensuing
five
years
of
no
sex
was
true

marital
bliss
because
she
was
already
married
to
grass
while
my
love
had
always
been
white
lines
of
coke

Condoms

condoms
are something that can both hurt
and help a high school reputation.

definitely helps the jock around
his Monday morning locker
as he quotes his conquests
at the drive-in the Saturday prior

but hurts the girl he dated
and did not screw but only
hung the condom
on the speaker at the drive-in
for all his buddies to see
a flag of conquest
that his buddies would defend
even though it was a false flag.

none of the guys cared
and the girls had no response
because in those days
most of them wished they had sex
and might even have lied to their
girlfriends in hopes of going
to the prom because they were hot.

so the condom is a powerful weapon
after months of wear it made
a clear image in the back pocket
of every guy's levis
only to be replenished by a new one

from the corner Texaco gas station
just waiting for the dual role of
having sex or maybe not and just hanging
on the drive-in speaker as if it did.

<u>The Corvette</u>

The
Corvette
was
only
a
year
old
and
candy
apple
red
parked
somewhere
on
the
coast
of
Oregon
near
Seaside
supposedly
only
one
hundred
dollars
and
for
sale
cheap
because
a

man
died
inside
and
was
not
found
for
many
years
and
the
smell
of
death
remained
and
could
not
be
removed
so
we
went
to
the coast
in
search
of
the
Vette
without
an

address
or
phone
number
because
we
were
sure
it
was
true
as
were
all
the
others
we
met
then
returned
home
not
defeated
we
knew
it
existed
somewhere
and
our
parents
did
not

243

criticize
at
our
first
encounter
with
an
urban
myth
like
the
rat
in
KFC
bucket
at
the
drive-in
movie

<u>A One-Legged Child</u>

a
one
legged
child
goes
to
a
playground
to
play
but
finds
that
the
playground
is
for
two
legged
kids
not
the
one
legged
child
who
wants
to
play
like
the

others
with
two
legs
but
I
do
not
care
I
am
booking
a
flight
to
Las Vegas
to
forget
about
the
one
legged
children
in
need
of
help

<u>The Panty Collector</u>

a
misshapen
face
which
he

covered
with
a
clown
mask
and

lived
deep
in
the
woods
where

no
one
could
see
him
take

off
his
mask
which

he
wore

when
he
drove
his
ice
cream

truck
and
lured
the
little
girls

with
his
music
and
free
dilly

bars
in
exchange
for
their
panties

which

he
sold
on
the
internet

to
raise
enough
money
for
a

trip
to
Japan
where
little
girls

used
panties
are
legally
sold
in

vending
machines
on
the
city
streets

to
lonely
men
afraid
to
steal

their
own
daughter's
used
stained
panties

The Exit

the
exit
is
where
I
entered
life
not
the
front
door
of
birth
which
explains
my
numerous
mishaps
and
quest
for
a
rebirth
beyond
the
gatekeeper
of
hell

Laughter

laughter
fades
fast
if
nobody
listens
my
friend
Norene
said
one
evening
long
ago
and
it
takes
two
to
enjoy
laughter
for
just
as
one
has
to
laugh
the
other
has

to
listen
to
make
a
laugh

<u>Yellow Grass</u>

yellow grass
was
the
time
of
year
the
buffalo
people
went
into
the
mountains
with
their
buffalo
it
was
cool
there
but
their
arrows
would
not
fly
true
due
to
the
trees

so
they
were
easily
killed
by
the
other
people
who
wore
beavers
on
their
heads
and
backs
and
had
smoking
sticks
but
still
the
buffalo
people
and
the
buffalo
died
cool

<u>Dirt On a Coffin</u>

dirt
on
a
coffin
makes
a
hallowed
sound
to
everyone
but
the
corpse
who
is
more
interested
in
death
than
the
sound
of
shovels
above
filling
his
grave
whom
everyone
above
will

soon
forget
but
the
worms
will
remember
as
the
crowd
dissipates
and
goes
home
to
shed
their
funeral
clothes
have
a
drink
turn
on
the
TV
and
not
really
give
a
shit
who

died
just
as
long
as
it
was
not
them

Unspoken

unspoken
are
the
many
words
we
forgot
to
say
at
a
loved
ones
funeral
or
memorial
I
suffer
daily
from
not
speaking
sooner
to
my
parents
about
questions
I
had
but

thought
I
had
forever
to
speak
and
sadly
time
ran
out
before
I
had
planned
and
I
am
left
with
only
murmurs
of
what
I
really
wanted
to
say
to
them
I
still

have
hope
each
and
every
time
I
see
an
eagle
soar
or
the
smell
of
a
long
lost
pipe
and
it
is
then
I
realize
they
are
still
here
and
with
me

always
as
I
sit
here
with
a
mouth
full
of
words
left
unspoken

Juggling Life

juggling life
between
two
shrinks
is
not
easy
especially
when
one
shrink
is
dating
your
wife
and
she
just
found
out
how
much
you
have
lied
as
did
she
but
salvation
is

in
my
other
shrink
whom
I
am
dating
to
no
surprise
to
anyone
who
knows
both
of
me

<u>Getting Even</u>

getting even
with
a
cheating
girlfriend
from
my
experience
is
to
marry
her
immediately
and
make
both
your
lives
miserable
I
thought
but
she
kept
on
cheating
and
I
continued
to
be

miserable
as
I
waited
for
the
sun
to
come
up
and
hopefully
hear
the
sound
of
her
car
tires
on
the
gravel
of
our
driveway
flat
tire
she
said
as
she
put
on

her
pajamas
while
wiping
the
white
coke
flakes
off
her
nose
and
said
I
love
you

<u>An Old Kitchen Table</u>

an old kitchen table
listens
today
as
it did
so many
years
ago
scarred
scratched
by many
childhood
memories
polished
by
dreams
and
elbows
of our
youth
it has
the
ability
to heal
just
by
being
a
table
like
a

grandparent
who
also
heals
by
their
aging
the
table
does
not
need
a cloth
or
special
lighting
it
just
needs
to
be
a
table
in
the
kitchen
of
someone
who
cares
about
the
table

like
me
and
mom

<u>The Cat</u>

The cat
in
my
life
is not
mine
really
he
appears
each
and
every
day
in
my
backyard
around
noon
and
sleeps
either
on
or
under
my
lawn chair
depending
upon
the
weather
I

see
him
when
I
leave
and
again
when
I
return
even
though
I've
never
fed
him
or
allowed
him
inside
where
I
live
sometimes
lonely
and
he
makes
me
not
lonely
so
I

named
him
Harvey
when
I
return
and
come
out
the
garage
door
he is
lying
there
back
against
the
door
welcoming
me
whom
he
does
not
know
but
apparently
trusts
as
he
follows
me

to
the
back
door
which
I
open
while
he
crawls
between
the
screen
door
and
back
door
and
sleeps
but
he is
always
gone
by
dark
maybe
just
maybe
I
will
feed
him
tomorrow

so he
is
less
hungry
and
I
am
less
lonely
shouldn't
do
it
really
but
I
love
him
like
no
other
wife
I
have
ever
had

The Closet

the closet
of
a fat
man
is
never
seen
by
another
less
fatter
than
he
it
holds
a
king's
ransom
in
clothing
of
varied
size
from
small
to
XXL
yet
only
one
size

seems
to
fit
the
others
however
will
constantly
be
tried
on
and
not
in
front
of
a
mirror
but
in
shame
and
defeat
thankfully
in
private
but
with
little
hope
of
ever
being

anything
different
or
much
anything
else
it
seems
today

Open Coffin

open coffin
when
not
permitted
due to
a kill
shot
in the
face
is every
Mafioso's
nightmare
to die
unrecognized
in a
closed
casket
not
even a
mother
can
open
to peek
inside
to see
a
son
who
no longer
exists
except

in
the
mortician's
handiwork
and
mafia
lore
do I
want to
die
that way
not sure
really
never been
in the
mafia
and no
longer
have a
mother

Free Lunch

free lunch
I tried
to
arrange
a
neighborhood
picnic
but
a
neighbor
superseded
both
me
and
everyone
else's
attempt
at a
neighborhood
party
this one
had
steaks
open
bar
backyard
table
seating
linen
china
live

music
and
nearly
everything
else
to make
it a
successful
party
I brought
my wine
and
vegetable
plate
for the
hostess
who
distracted
attended
to her
imbibing
and
hungry
minions
but
not I
who
left
as
steaks
were
served
knowing

very
well
there
was
no
such
thing
as
a
free
lunch

<u>Art</u>

art
is
something
I have
learned
to fear
frightening
beyond
all
imagination
for
the
artist
has
to tell
the
truth
to
all
who will
listen
each
art
work
reveals
to the
public
the
soul
of the
artist

who
himself
does
not yet
understand
his
own
soul
which
makes
the
fear
so
much
greater

<u>Carnival</u>

Carnival
of
dysfunction
is
where
idiots
play
the
cost
is
free
nothing
works
it
is
all
broken
by
those
who
don't
care
and
do
not
come
into
the
tent
to
see

light-bulb
digesters
sword
swallowers
regurgitation
specialists
and
a
room
where
men
lift
weights
with
their
penis
for
all
to
see
if
they
paid
tariff
to
the
masters
who
sleep
outside
the
tents
safe

and
dream
of
more
gimps
born
under
their
tents

<u>Silence</u>

silence
of
all
the
little
ones
to
weak
to
cry
tears
often
alone
from
hunger
thirst
discarded
by
mothers
to
weak
to
nurse
without
milk
but
only
dust
laden
shriveled
brown

teats
useless
in
the
hot
afternoon
African
sun
lying
on
the
ground
along
a
dirt
path
to
nowhere
too
low
to
be
hit
by
bullets
but
occasionally
run
over
by
rebel
trucks
to

experience
at
last
peace

<u>Happiness</u>

today
I was
happy
for the
first
time
in
decades
I was
reading
lying
on my
bed
on a
warm
Saturday
afternoon
looking
out
my
window
watching
the
leaves
of a
tree
illuminated
by the
sun
golden
and

waving
at
me
as
I
dozed
off
no
planes
trains
birds
or
car
sounds
for
an
hour
or
so
not
sure
I
deserved
such
but
I
sure
felt
good
when
I
awakened
happily
and
surprised

<u>The Fly</u>

the fly
on
the wall
of a
cell
full of
frogs
does not
have
much
chance
for
parole
or
escape
for
that
matter
so
it
stayed
still
high
on the
wall
of
the
cell
away
from
darting

tongues
then
flew
down
to
the
floor
to let
the frogs
fight
each
other
over
it
then
flew
away
high
on
the
wall
again
until
all
the
frogs
were
dead
then
it
flew
down
to

295

feast
on
the
frogs
paroled
at
last

Suicide Motel

suicide motel
with no
returns
the sign
said
or
in red
neon
on the
roof
of
a
roadside
motel
abandoned
I
thought
as I
drove by
hurriedly
escaping
from
my
own
sorrows
and such
I drove
70 mph
up
the
freeway

towards
nowhere
in
particular
when
I saw
a
wreck
and
body
bags
strewn
on a
wet
pavement
when
I
remembered
the motel
and thought
just maybe
they
did not
want
to die
as
I do
almost
every
day
from
dusk
until

a
very
early
dawn
a
dawn
that
was
always
dark
it
seemed
thinking of
the
suicide
motel
I
did a
U turn
back
towards
the motel
I
checked in
at the
customer
service
counter
never
to be
heard
from
again

hopefully
to
save
one
of
those
at the
wreck site
I
just
passed
people
who really
wanted to
live
as much
as I
want
to die
the room
was nice
and
I fell
asleep
forever
finally
happy
and not
fat

<u>The Direction</u>

the direction
I know
for sure
but often
it is
two steps
forward
and
one back
but
the
destination
I still
do not
know
and
maybe
never will
because
I forget
so easily
each day
about
what
I am
to do
and
what
I have
done
and

where
I
have
been
lost
I
guess
forever
it
seems
forever
and
ever
in
the mist
called
old age
I
suppose
but
I
do not
remember
if I'm
old
or
still
young
maybe
I guess

<u>Joy</u>

joy
is
something
I
do not
think
about.
more
often
it is
in
my art
and
those
around
me.
people
say
so.
if you
are
listening
Val
this
poem
is
for
you.

Abandonment

abandonment
is
something
horrible
we
all
know
because
who
abandons
a baby
left
on a
hospital
porch
or
a puppy
left
in the
rain
on
a curb
or
a child
to
crack
discarded
parents
still
it is
abandonment

a long
word
never
the less
but the
act
is
repulsive
and
those
who cause
the crime
are
just as
guilty
as
those
who
abandon

Suicide

suicide
is
wonderful
if
planned
properly
with
no one
looking
or
knowing
when
it will
take place
morning
noon
or
night
does
not
matter
really
dead
is
the same
no matter
what
time
of
day
trust me

I
have
been
there
before
dead
that is

Arnold Swarzensquirrel

arnold swarzensquirrel
woke up one day
pissed off
at all
the cars
whizzing by
below
his nest
I have had it
he said
and just then
decided
to fight back
and become
strong
pull ups
from
tree limbs
crushing
nuts
between
his paws
pushups
no way
unfortunately
his feet
were
positioned
wrong
day
after day

month
after month
he continued
to work out
until
one day
he felt
strong
enough
to
take on
the cars
the day
was rainy
as he laid
in the street
his back fur
wet
he shivered
but
not afraid
as he
heard it
approach
the wheel
touching
his tail
he flexed
with
all
his might
and
pushed

with feet
and paw
against
the car's
tire
until
it
flipped over
and
he ran
up into
his tree
and
watched
from his nest
as police
ambulance
a fire truck
all gathered
below
not knowing
the squirrel
did not care
if
anyone lived
or
all
were dead
across the street
he looked
and saw a
bigger tree
with no nest
but maybe
a gym

The Cowboy

the cowboy
sits
high
on
his horse
looking
for
yesterday
without
a barbed wire
fence
and
the cattle
also
looked
for
a day
without
a fence
and
but were
saddened
as
was the horse
the cowboy
rode
to watch
the proud
cowboy
dismount
to unlatch

the gate
in
the
shinny new
fence
after
he rode
through
it was
not locked
his horse
looked back
as
the cattle
came through
so much
for the west
our cowboy
once knew
but
he went to bed
that night
smiling
giggling
inside

<u>The Rose</u>

the rose
is a rose
and
the nose
is a nose
everyone
knows
but
does the rose
smell
the nose
like the nose
smells
the rose
only the pedals
know
and
I can't hear
them talk
to let me
know
but softly
they wave
on
the early nights
breeze
waving to me
I want to know
the answer
to the riddle
above

but I'm
in a hurry
to go
to the gym
and
the rose
will be there
forever
as it always
has been
so when
I have time
I will listen
to the
rose

Resume to God

resume to god
bless me father
for I am
still sinning
and
it has been
51 years
since my last
confession
I am sure
you know
about
high
unemployment
down here
the homeless
our wars
burning
synagogues
churches
and mosques
we don't seem
to like peace
anymore
because we cannot
afford it
the economy is bad
so I am going
to get a jump
on all the others
and submit my resume

for a place
on your team
do embellishments
count against me
I hope not
my life has been such
but
hurting others
I no longer do
don't go to church
nor hell do I want
nor bother you
with prayers
full of want
no
it's just a place
in heaven
that I do
now seek
based on this resume
not on my past
but where do I post it
on which site
surely not
facebook
too many already
there
seeking redemption
resumes in hand
but not I
who's going
to mail it
to you
snail mail
with a stamp

The Milkman Dropped Dead on the Porch

the milkman dropped dead on the porch
as he ran from our house
on cherry street
to his red and white truck
still idling
in the chill
of a late fall morning

not from the weight
of the milk bottles
but rather
my father came home
two hours early
and found him

white uniform discarded
in clumps
on the kitchen floor
while we were at school
forced to drink milk
by the nuns

we never knew
but my father did
and
we were never allowed
to drink milk
from the cow again

Iceberg Wife

iceberg wife
is not a pretty poem
or
even a nice one
but still
it happened
on a drunken night
at Dukes
a bar
on lower Queen Anne
Avenue
in Seattle
during the early 80's
booze with coke
fake Rolex watches
money no problem
when I met her
stunning
and with large breasts
I fell in love
and spent a fortune
which never ended
during our marriage
then
and beyond
at first
her body fooled me
it lay like an iceberg
at dukes
that first night
70% below the surface
but not the tits

Don't Drag a Cannon Uphill

don't drag a cannon uphill
as the ghosts
of previous battles
would attest
because they know well
that
we are not invisible
in the dead world
and, it will be futile
considering the dust
sweat
manpower
only to find out
the enemy
held the high ground
before you
the battle
already lost
the canon is not human
after all

The Lion and the Frog

The lion and the frog
did not know each other
but
both roared at night
one from the treeless plains
the other
from a drying up pond
not knowing each other
wasn't a problem
they'd heard each other
many times
a fearless roar
and an equally fearless croaks
when they finally met
by the edge of the pond
the lion did not roar
and the frog
did not croak
neither afraid
but could not help each other
during the drought
and hot winds
that dried the pond
the lions water
and the frogs home
so they finally met
muzzle to nose
not knowing what came next
the lion's nose
touching the water
the frogs tongue

touching the lion's nose
and they smiled
one croaked
the other roared
while droplets of water
fell from the lion's whiskers
onto the frog's tongue
Okay is this happy?
If so I want to get back
to my next poem titled,
"Blood looks black under a full moon!"

Black Beauty

was a bat
I never knew her
but my friend did
his father showed him
each night
just before bed

she was hickory
34 inches in length
just like the real ones
which hit baseballs
out of a ball park
but not his

his father's
black beauty
did not hit balls
but broke bones
that kept the boy
out of school

until his bruises
and scabs
healed
to convince the teacher
that he fell
and was just clumsy

but one day
in the midst
of a cold winter

the handle of the bat
reversed
and the boy was "at bat"

he killed his father
a home run at last
out of the ball park
and he cried
in the chair
kind of cool
and no-one cared

The Point

the point
a place I never wanted to be
feeling for mines
not yet IED's
of a modern war
I did not yet know
but still he walked forward
towards where we did not know
over paddies
and marshes
to protect us one and all
my wounds have long healed
the point's have not
because he is always
in front of the troops
just being a point
who's fate we did not know
until a villager told us
we had lost a friend
who meant nothing to them
but so much to me

Please Die in a War

Please die in a war
the corpsman said
and do not be wounded
in the chest
with a sucking wound
that necessitates care
of many others
who have to leave combat
to take care of you
for a fault not your own
but statistics do not fail
for every wounded
three must depart front lines
to take care of you
so please die
and hope the enemy shoots straight
to save us all the problem
of trying to save you
when we just want to go home
and away from a battle
we do not understand
the corpses are stacked
away from view
no flags on a body bags
but later on a coffin
and then in review
for only loved ones
and those who do not care
about a war
in a foreign place
in the news

that interrupts
Jeopardy
on TV
enough said
because I am alive
who writes about battle
but does not feel the hurt
of today's soldier
my battles are past

Sounds

Sounds
they do not become me
but no one listens
to my plea
for silence
without killing
the noisemakers
I am not kidding when I say
noise of any kind
drives me nuts
and angry
almost ready to kill
the source of the sound
be it bird
train
airplane
or, automobile
most of all
a chained dog's pleading
I hate them all
they ruin my life
but,
I do not know where to go
to escape
from more than a nuisance
you think I am kidding
about my level of distraught
I surely am not
I have sought counseling
and bought machines
to cover the noise

if that makes me insane
then the pain is real
to hear the train go
where it must
the airplane take off
as it should
and the robin sing
to the drip of my faucet
but I hate them all
and hide in my nest
with white noise machines
and fans
to hide the noise
that drives me crazy
someday I will silence them all

The 3<u>rd</u> Grade Clock

there is nothing slower
than a classroom clock
just before recess
or lunch break
or end of school
it was not a clock really
but a presence
we could not control
nor could the nuns
who taught us
it just ticked away
the arm
clicking backwards
before it clicked forward
and advanced a minute
a precious minute to us
all who watched
impatiently
nodding off
it could not go fast enough
but we had been there before
waiting
anxiously
as the clocked ticked
loudly it seemed
and made or life happy
or sad
when it clicked too slow
it seemed
but it clicked the same
whether recess

or lunch
Or going home
we tried to change it once
but got caught
by the lady in black and white
who admonished us all
not knowing the brave culprit
who put back the arms
with a yard stick
as we all watched in awe
Dennis was his name
and braver than us he surely was
but the nun came back too soon
and Dennis was caught
we all held or breath
for once
the clock seemed to stop
as Dennis was paddled
in front of us all

The Puppy

The Puppy
was quite little
as a puppy should be
he sat by the road
wishing for food
from a passing car
I was not driving
when the pup darted
and crossed the road
and ran before our car
a Cuban rental
with not good brakes
when we struck him
he bounced into the gulley
beside the road
we did not stop
nothing to do
just another black dog
no one wanted to feed
whose life ended
on some dusty road
the people so poor
that a puppy's life
did not matter
when everyone starved
on government rations
the dog got none
but he was not told
that life would difficult
and he'd have to find food
with no mother or father

and risks
what he did not know
we drove on
in silence
no time for sarcasm
about the thud under our car
about how sad it was
for a black puppy
which we did not know

The Escalator

the escalator
in an airport in south Africa
all seemed quite normal
polished chrome
going up and down
to awaiting flights
but she changed it all
black as she was
she descended before me
and said hello before her fall
she fell on a step
and the escalator kept running
of course it did
it had no mind of its own
as the lady stumbled
and fell to the step
she looked at me in anguish
with fear in her eyes
as her coat was caught
between the escalator steps
she reached to touch me
I was not afraid to respond
she was pinned and quite scared
by the revolving steps
that tore into her back
her coat hat been caught
but no one cared
about the blood dripping
from her coat
still no one cared
because she was black

and the year before tutu
Mandela still in jail
I dropped what I carried
and descended the steps
I pulled her bloodied coat lose
and she grabbed me close
and pissed on my leg
her blood on my blue blazer
her pain still within
the both of us
I comforted her
because no one else cared
an injured black
they had seen it before
there was nothing I could do
as I boarded my plane
I wondered how she suffered
to wherever she went
one person at boarding
said just one word
Kaffirs
that's all
they do not care
about suffering
or hurt
as he ordered a drink

My War

I wish I had a war
to call all my own
from which to return from
on the front steps
of mom and dad's home
where I was raised
a war that was popular
and publicly acclaimed
like that of my father
who wore his uniform in pride
not like the one
I attempted to hide
I remember crossing the bridge
between the airport and home
stopping dad's car
and opened the trunk
to throw out my seabag
into the river below
it did not feel good
or bad in fact
just something I had to do
to come home once more
and not feel the taint
of an unpopular war
it was some year later
that I realized a war
and was wounded in the process
as if to settle a score
for what I did not do
in the Vietnam war

A Rat in My Shoe

a rat in my shoe
was not a good sign
as I woke up in my flat
so cold that the rat
found refuge in the heat
of my discarded slipper
but no one else did
I never had visitors to
my chilly domain
full of art
some my own
and a dire sense of failure
that was also my own
and I did not
inherit it
I created it myself
as I fell down
the stairs of my life
and never seemed
to get up
just like the rat
who died
in my slipper
one cold night

<u>Mother Nature</u>

I looked out my window and
watched a crow grasp the tail
of a squirrel in its beak
the squirrel's small feet churned
the grass for traction
but the crow won and the squirrel's
tail came off in the crow's mouth
and it ran to the nearest tree
slowly bleeding to death
as the crow took flight
dropping the squirrel's tail in the
uppermost branches
after all what use does a crow have
with a bloody squirrel's tail

we were steelhead fishing
my dad and I when we saw it
the snake and the frog in a battle
in which the snake appeared
to be winning but the frog had other
ides and used its forelegs to keep the snake
from swallowing it whole
we walked downstream for a mile or so
caught some big fish and build
a camp ground for the night
where we cooked the fish
early the next morning just before dawn
I hiked back up the river to where I had
last seen the snake and the frog
they were both very still
in their deadly embrace

I cried late into the night about
the dog we all loved
who had swum out into the river
to see a raccoon which taunted him
by standing on a rock in the middle
of a fast moving river
but the dog did not know that the river was deep
and the raccoon was fooling him
as barney approached the rock we all yelled
to dissuade him to no avail
he wanted the taunting raccoon
who was much smarter and as the dog
approached the raccoon grabbed his head
with its sharp front claws
and turned the dog towards him and downstream
from the rock into the fast current
barney tired after a while and we quite yelling
as his golden body floated down the river
and the raccoon swam away to the farther shore
the two yellow eyes watched from the dark of the forest
as the campers set up their tent and started a campfire
cooked their meal as they sat around their table
the body with the yellow eyes launched itself
and ran to the tent where he had watched the little
girl who cried when she squeezed it
he took it into his mouth and ran into the dark woods
on the other side of the camp
without anyone seeing it and the girl
who never knew what happened to the doll

She Said Call Anytime

she said call anytime
and I did
and it was
fun until
one day I found
myself married
not to her
but my phone
which I used
every night
to call
someone else
and in those days
minutes
were not free
cell phones
did not exist
so it was
the land line
that got me caught
and the bill
oh well
now I have a
cell phone
and the minutes
are almost
free
in comparison
but
I have no one
to call

339

and no one
to even
cheat on
nor
entice
damn

She Left Me at Hello

she left me at hello
and never
looked
back
as far as
I know
it was over
until
many years
later
when I read
in the paper
that she had
killed
her husband
and son
with a hatchet
as they slept
and then
tried to kill
herself
by hanging
from a shower
rod
which every
suicidal person
knows for a
fact
is too flimsy
to accomplish such
I got a call from jail

asking for money
for a bail which
she would never see
but read later
she was in prison
and I hope
being sodomized
by all the dykes
surrounding her
cot
all sweaty
with tattoos
they wanted
to share
while they
rubbed up
against her
in the throes
of meaningless
prison sex
she was home
at last
behind the bars
she deserved
or maybe did not

The Marine

the Marine
of the sixties
was a very strange breed
first of all
he is a volunteer
where others were not
he got drunk
in Oceanside
and bought a ring
for a girl he just met
and wanted
to marry
before he went to Nam
which his girl did not know
was a lover killer
sure as hell and
she would not be there
when and if
he returned
but the ring
surely hocked while
he was in battle
dodging bullets
while she picked out
another ring
from another Marine
but still all Marines
are best friends
not the people back
home
who did not go through

boot camp
have their heads shaved
and humiliated before each dawn
but after a short while
letters from home
became their best friends
and then they left
to places unknown
where they
either survived or
were killed
just a body count really
unless yours was killed
no other options were
there were
except the wounded
who were forgotten
by those still alive
who could no longer fought sailors
in the bathrooms
of the San Diego Airport
where all Marines
earned their stripes
before they were awarded
in battles to come
but to beat up a sailor
was a badge
of courage
until the purple hearts
started running red
from all the Marines
I have forgotten
except one time a year
in November
that is

The Indian

the Indian
I saw in my
rear view mirror
was lying in a dusty ditch
just along the highway
and I barely felt the
bump against my
reinforced bumper
and grill
but that is another story
I do remember I was
reaching for a beer
when I hit him and
he flew ten feet into the air
and over my 1976
Cadillac Eldorado convertible
cherry red in color
mark one up for Custer
I look both forwards and back
and saw no other drivers
so I was safe for now
just another drunken Indian
seeking a short cut to
the happy hunting grounds
in a road side ditch
to most passersby
he pushed on the gas pedal
and thought about how
this shitty day began
in a hot and steamy court house
in El Paso for a divorce settlement

for which he did not care
as he ran to the garage at recess
never to return
his back seat full of clothes now
flapping in the wind
his truck full of things he no longer
cared about but meant something
to her
she got the house with the
cracked pool
yard full of colorful plastic furniture
and a car that barely run
at least until he put sugar in her gas tank
so here he now was
racing down the highway toward
Tucson with parts of an Indian on his
reinforced grill and bumper
which he learned about
when he was illegally transporting
stolen cars from Nicaragua
to el Salvador during the contra
war and beyond
he pushed on towards the west
and a soon to be setting sun
when he saw them
hundreds of them
Mexicans
crouching by the side of the road
Clorox bottles full of water
hanging from their belts
targets as in a pin ball game
dodging traffic
heading to the nearest taco bell

no match
for his reinforced grill
nor the beers he had beside him
mere bugs on a bumper
on a hot desert night

The Pet

I do not like pets
of any kind
dogs, cats, or almost
anything else
except for the
gold fish
but
when I think about
it
I would not want myself
for a pet either
I am always hungry
need a bath once in a
while
and the more you feed me
the more I crap but at least
in a toilette
of someone else's invention
but still
I would not want me
for a pet
I do think
because I would not come
when called
or even chase a ball
and would want my
teeth washed
as so many humans do
and watch television
and not curl up
but sit in a chair

by the fire and demand
popcorn and other such
no not even I
could ever become a pet
except maybe
a gold fish
which does not have to
make its own bed
but then I
do not even know
if gold fish have a
bed to make

The Egret

the egret
I saw today
flying over Vancouver lake
was most likely
the most beautiful thing
I have ever seen.

It was a complete surprise
as I parked by the shore
to figure out my life
which was a task
next to impossible
it must have heard me
for it took off in a rush
of splendor
snow white winds dipped
just over the water
orange and black beak
partially open as if to
gather air at take off
but of course
I do not really know
its white feathered body
framed against the dark green
of the trees
its feet tucked back
under a black tail
relaxing until the next
landing when the feathers
will become heavy with water
and turn gray

until dried
but to me he was a spirit
of sorts
who made me forgot
for just
a moment

Dinka Wood

dinka wood
is what we called them
after they were shot
or bodies burned
by blazing tire necklaces

that's just the way it was
back then
as we stacked their
even more blackened bodies
in a pile with gasoline
to light
and put the monkey people
asunder

that's just the way it was
back then
at least as I remember it
they came from the cover
of the tobacco fields
which employed us
just fresh from Vietnam
and other foreign wars
we were young and
billeted in a fine hotel
and did not lack the least
except for a few KIAs
but it ended after a year
when we lost by a truce
that sent us all home
and the country soon became

a jungle with blacks
ruling whites
and blacks killing whites
and blacks
because they didn't know
much else but to fight
and starve as a tribe
while I look at my very own
dinka wood trophy hanging
on the wall of the den

a heat rippled record
in a case that merely said
Rhodesians never die
and the monkeys always
will kill themselves

The Banana

a true story about me
at my worst and my best
new years eve 1964

we went to a buddy's house
parents gone of course
three cases of old English 800
later I went under the table

glass topped it was
and very expensive
from now on it is a story told
by others because I did not
remember a thing as I crawled
under the table and asked
three of my buddies to sit atop

and on a fateful debt
I would lift it up
with all atop
I did and the glass broke but
no one was hurt except for
for Greg's mom's table
which disintegrated
in glass particles all around
me as I received the hero's
Viking toast which I did not also
remember not anything about
early onset Alzheimer's
but was a very early beer expert
who was put in the trunk of a car

and dropped off on my parent's porch
with a banana in my ass
they pushed the door bell around
two o'clock or so and left me
on my knees with the very same
banana in my ass
dad came to the door
of this remember because of the
fear factor
put me on the living room couch
pulled up my pants and I awakened
surrounded by three curious sisters
watching the rose bowl parade
never yet realizing that their brother
would soon be sent to the battlefields
of Vietnam while all his friends stayed
home but I still like bananas
today but always check the label
to be sure it was not mine

A Contortionist

a contortionist
is not always twisted
but just looks such to
all those twisted
who watch him in his act
on a stage

in a forlorn circus
where the tents are
tattered and faded
and the animals ribs show
with near starvation

but the show must go on
fat lady or not
the bearded lady left
months ago with the
strong man who nightly
lifted foam bar bells

but the midget
was still there
taking tickets
from people
who never appear
but still remember
a circus
of their youth

when the lions roared
and still had sharp teeth

but the contortionist
carried on nightly
to an audience of one

until one night
he stole the sword swallowers
sword and ate it
just after a dinner

of the sharp-edged tickets
the circus never sold
gagged and swallowed
not the sword
which was in his belly

<u>My Destination</u>

my destination
always seems to be hidden
in the folds of some map
of which I cannot read
not see where I have been
nor where I am going

I do know I can't go back
I have already been there
and I have too much pain
to be dead so I must be
somewhere

so I took a few too many
pills and drinks and entered
the mirror maze
and never was able
to come back

but I finally found
my destination
but it was all black
with no sun
to tan me as l like

A Redneck Wedding

a redneck wedding
doesn't last more than a minute
and is discussed on a tattered
couch in an yard full of leaves
just outside a rusty and tilting

trailer full of a wife and kids
the grooms hiding from
their recent guilt
for raping a disoriented tourist

seeking her parent's cabin
for a month's respite
from the hot and crowded city
who mistakenly stopped at their

gas station and asked directions
only to find too much help
from those who did not really
want to help at all

but who should live in fear
for she who knew much about
a women scorned
and vengeance

upon those
who scorned her and
for until
death do us part

Before the Last Snow Falls

before the last snow falls
was my mother's wish
but not my father's
he had seen his share of
snowfalls as a kid in Iowa
and did not want to see
anymore

which was irrelevant since
he had already passed
away leaving mom alive
under the snowflakes
we both enjoyed immensely
until she also expired

but still the snowflakes fell
on school yards, roadways
and other minor
inconveniences
which were not much
inconvenient to those

who could not sit at home
drinking away the melted
snowflakes of my misspent
youth and a bottle
of vodka chilled in a freezer
as the ads said it was supposed

to be in the ads in GQ and other
publications until my money

ran out and the house got cold
with ice crystals on the inside
on my bedroom windows which
I broke with a rock in despair

The Last Train Home

the last train home
is what my grandfather
called it in his stories to
me as a boy eager for any
of his tales about
his time in Russia building
the Trans-Siberian railroad

in 1916 we finished he said
and showed me an old photo
of himself in a rickshaw on
the great wall of china festooned
in a Pershing military cap and
not one but two crossed pistols

on a full bandolier laded with
bullets, youth and enthusiasm
I still have that photo in the
original Chinese frame along
with two Cloisonné vases from
the last emperor of china

and late at night when grandmother
was asleep he showed me another
faded but very risqué photo of himself
and a very large Russian lady
naked half immersed in the warm
waters of Lake Baikal and he showed
it only to me with one warning

but the memories of the last
trains home bothered him forever
they were box cars loaded with
frozen bodies of Russian soldiers
prisoners and Chinese who had died
under his supervision and not all of

the cigar and pipe smoke he exhaled
each day could not rid him of these
memories even though he was a most
gentle pie on the windowsill during the
depression kind of Irish gentleman whom
everyone liked and respected most of all

he became head of a railroad and we kids
had our own private car to tour at our
pleasure with his guidance never realizing
that this our fun car would also be my
grandfathers last train home to join those
he buried so many years ago for progress

What Would I Do

what would I do
in a drinker's
morning bar
in Rock Springs
Wyoming along
the railroad
tracks
with an hangover
and a young girl
with the biggest
tits in town and
a sweater that
revealed them
to anyone who
looked
and they all did
as we entered the
bar with empty
glasses and a
early morning thirst
or was it last nights
hangover that wanted
to fill the glass
left over from the
five dollar a night
campground
interrupted by bears
who ate the drugs and
broke the last bottle
as we cowered
not thinking of a drink

until morning which
just arrived sooner
than we thought
as we sit in this
booth in a dive
by the railroad
called the hard time
café which did not
have a nice ring to it
we ordered and they
looked and taunted
as I planned my exit
before the food
even arrived
I checked out the
men's room and
found no escape there
without her
I was scared
but young and tough
like any Marine back
from Vietnam when I
knew they were not
so I merely did as
instructed and moved
first and a broken nose
was all it needed to gain
our freedom not my nose
but something my father
taught before the drill
instructors
to strike first
is all it takes

to part a crowd and
make a getaway
to another depressing
campground
with someone I did
not like and who was
danger to myself
and all those who
followed after me
in a double wide

Shot Dead

shot dead
means nothing more
than what the coroner
says is true not the
medics and ER docs
who still think you are
alive and can be saved
but when the cops put
your chalk outline on a
floor or pavement they
know you are truly and
forever dead and do not
really care
about another body
full of bullets and blood
on the few gloves they
have to expend this
rainy city night when
they could be home safe
from the chalk marks
on the sidewalks washing
down the sidewalks
outside their dismal
apartments
in a city which does not
care as long as the bodies
are shot dead and do not
come back to haunt them
from a court
or
from jail

Jimmy the Kangaroo

jimmy the kangaroo
woke up one hot morning
as he always did covered
with dust and hungry
but something was very
different this time
his feet were chained to
a jeep and he did not
remember how he got here
alone on the desert somewhat
like home but it was not
there were loud sounds
and people crying all around
but still he was hungry
and wanted to sleep and
get away from this horrible
place of loud sounds and very
dark people who carried guns
like totems back home that
the little black people carried
but this was different and he
knew it because he heard them
saying it was his big feet they
really wanted to jump across
the sands of wherever he was
to detect something he did not
know bombs they were called
so they fed him well and set
him about his way with his big
feet in motion to do something
he did not know until he

heard a sound and fell back
and felt pain as he saw his
his feet in the sand behind
him and heard a person say
throw him in the ditch and
get us another roo

A Broken Window

a broken window
was all I saw in my youth
it never got fixed because
I did not know how
and mom and whomever
did not care because their
window was fine
I watched the snow flakes
come into my room via the
broken window and melt
on my tattered army blanket
which covered me as a
child but not now
in a warm and dry summer
the crickets also came into
my broken window
and sleep with me to make
sure I was not alone
and I thanked them
by going to the broken window
wand pulling out a jagged
piece of glass not to kill myself
but to cut a hole in the
mattress in which I slept
and to keep me company
until another frigid winter
leaves me alone without
my cricket friends
which I will now follow
into the fields
that surround me

to where with only
a jagged piece of glass and
memories of where I thought
I was until I remembered
about where I had not been
as the crickets chirped
and the frogs croaked
to remind me

Ernie and the Rat

Ernie and the rat
is not a pleasant story
in any forum except a
theater of war when such
things happen in the dead
of night when a 19 year old
soldier earns his stripes
as I did under the cover
of fog and desperation as
young Ernie slept peacefully
inebriated by the Everclear
cocktails I fed him for an hour
until he passed out
not worrying by the dawn
that would never come
because the rats were all
he saw and felt when he
awakened in pain
never to be seen again by
me and my handiwork of
stuffing two Everclear laden
cotton balls as he slept
not worrying about the times
he let us down on guard
so the cotton balls were put
into his ears as he slept and
the last word I heard was that
he was brain damaged from
the rat's feast
never to be seen again
from us at least

who never sleep
while a war goes on
about us

Rain Drops

rain drops
are not a friend of mine
as they slowly drop from
a leaf and remind me of an
icicle dripping in slow
motion as I watch for the
dripping to end
like the dripping from the faucet
in my bathroom which keeps
me awake and causes me to
think about senseless poems
such as this which truly tests
my patience for all things not
bob which makes me realize
that I am alone in a world
that does not care about bob
nor Jim, Don and Tom because
to be noticed in this world
means one has to be either
a presidential killer or a
Nobel Laureate or some other
person who has made a name
for themselves by being a viral
sensation online and else where
but no I am just bob lost
within myself as I watch the
snowflakes dry on the hood
of my car as I drive it over
a cliff with eyes closed
not seeing the bottom
as others would see it

as death
but not
a redemption
of sorts
for the bob
I used to know

The Soup Can

the soup can
which I happened
to purchase just
happened to be tomato
as she wanted or so
she said to me in the
aisle of the grocery
I had just met her a
moment ago and fell
under her spell less
than a moment later
or maybe even sooner
by then I was already
under her spell
her betty page retro hair
wine red or maybe even
blood red should have
warmed me as was her
cadaver white skin which
had a sheen but not a shine
but I was too proud to be
with her as we approached
the check out with only
one can of soup in our hands
departing for home is where
the dream ended but only for

a moment and then we were
back at my place in the kitchen
where she took the top off the
can and licked the tomato with

a smile and said that she wanted
to get naked which was fine with
me never been with a goddess before
and most likely never will be again
she got naked and we went into the
bathroom and were seated before
the mirror when she straddled me
and put a towel around my neck and
said trust me as she gouged both my
cheeks with the raw metal edge of
the tomato and can got dressed while
I bled and merely said I like my men
with scars after all it is only tomato
juice as she turned and walked out
of my life forever and forever I will
seek her out because I had never been
in love like this before

The Frog

the frog
is not a pretty thing
as it sit on a lily pad
and croaks to no one
in particular but another
frog listens and answers
the first frog and he
jumps from his pad in
delight answering a croak
that never was it was
just another frogs echo
that he heard from across
the pond of his loneliness
just being a frog
when everyone on TV
seemed to be other than
a frog so he would hop
home and change from his
frog costume into what
he thought would be very
attractive but the more he
hopped to show off his outfit
the more he found out that
no one watched for after all
he was s just a frog who
wanted to be anything other
than a deep green frog
who would never leave his pond
afraid of what the next pond
would be like
always alone and only afraid
that the pond would dry up

Snow Fall

snow fall
is something I would
once again like to see
not in the mountains
but in my own driveway
and on my roof
just one more time
is all I ask before my
time runs out snowflakes
aplenty deafening sounds
of traffic and people
and pile high over my boots
and give me one last night
of sleep without worries
or nightmares with only
my head on a cool pillow
from the Wynn Hotel is all
I ever wanted and not be
scared about tomorrow
which I always feared
because I do not deserve
a peaceful tomorrow
and never will

The Robin

the robin
had a red breast
as they all do even
redder against the
green of dad's freshly
mowed lawn but he
would not sit still
in the sight of my new
Red Ryder BB gun as it
poked through the
tear in the screen
covering my bedroom
window so I had to
do what the cowboys did
and lick my finger and
touch my sight and hold
my breath and fire again
because I missed before
and shot the worm
dangling from the robins
mouth instead
but now my aim would
be straight and sure
just like in the movies
I saw on Saturday
before being kicked out
for throwing Sugar
Daddys that stuck to the
screen but now back to
the robin before mom
and dad came home

from I did not know
nor did I really care
just as long as it was
not before the robin
fell to the grass
I snuck out the back
door crept across the
lawn and approached
the bird which I soon
found out was not dead
so I closed my eyes
and shot him again to
stop his misery picked
him up to throw him
into the large holly tree
and out of sight but not
from the sight of my
approaching father back
from wherever and I
was caught and he only
said this is not duck
hunting which is a sport
what you did was not
a sport as you will
learn shortly
during a sleepless night
in which I found the robin
still and in the holly tree
I cradled him gently and
buried him in the garden
under a full moon the
same as the one now above
me in a fox hole in a war

in a foreign country and
truly wonder if the robin
was when I found out I
could kill which I am now
doing but not with a BB
gun but other persons
lives which we no longer
buried in a garden

The Tree

the tree
had many leaves
the last time I
remembered but
then I took a
drink after a long
time sober
and when I woke
up the tree had
no more leaves
and my room was
cold with no one
to care they had
been there before
so I clung to the
floor where I had
fallen at least with
my bottle within
reach but almost
empty so I wondered
how I got here alone
on my floor just
awaiting a drink for
ever more.

The Bathroom

the bathroom
behind a Mexican
cantina just south
of the border
in which I am in
had a filthy floor
a backed up toilet
and a sink that
was full of my blood
and a bloody shirt
I used as a bandage
instead of sutures
which I could not
afford and could not
report as a bullet
wound in my abdomen
would do me in as
they always said about
a stomach wound
I could not go home
because home was a
base across the border
for all of us Marines
who were warned not
to go on leave to
Tijuana no matter how
big her tits were in the
ad at the bus station
but still I went and had
too many drinks and
never saw her tits

nor the gun that fired
the bullet that put me
down on the floor of
the bathroom with only
a mongrel dog with
toilet paper stuck to its
paws licking my wound

<u>Waiting for Nightfall</u>

waiting for nightfall
beside a waterfall
without water
but only sand
flowing over the
rocks as the life
around it dies and
only leaves skeletal
remains to prove it
was even here
wherever here is
before the water
dried up and the sun
never set and we all
wait for a nightfall
which will not come
in my lifetime
nor that of the other
destitute who huddle in
the shade pretending
it was a nightfall
unlike the rich across
the river who are
merely wondering how
this drought and sunshine
will affect their next
harvest of the seasons
grapes which will be
served as wine at the
next party they hold in
their air-conditioned

and drought proof
mansions looming just
across the river as we
bath in the only moist
sand we can find and
and await nightfall
on the other side of
the shrinking river
shimmering in our
imaginations as a
mirage

Putting a Good Horse Down

putting a good horse down
is most difficult
to say the least
not like taking your
dog to the vet to
also to be put down
the horse has
made you a cowboy
and you were one
riding the range
herding cattle
and keeping you
sane on lonely nights
on the prairie when
chill winds blew
and snowflakes fell
on the both of you
when the camp fire
went out and the
embers were cold
and the Indians
arrows in both of us
festered and hurt
but we had to lay still
so as not to be
discovered
when I made my mistake
and looked in his eyes
milky and brown
and realized he was
suffering much more

then I and the Indians
be damned Chester was
in pain and we would
die not alone so I
pulled the trigger
and Chester lay still
as I huddled by his
body as the war hoops

began and

arrows started flying
many hit home

The Pillow

the pillow
has two sides
only one is cool
like the sheets
just taken off
the backyard
clothesline
both of which
will make up my
freshly made
Saturday nights
bed which I will
never share
not out of spite
but of fear and
mistrust of the
female scent
which has
followed me like
a cheap cologne
from my first
wedding to my
last divorce
but never did
she keep the
sheets
which revealed
my infidelity
on many occasions
when she came
home late at night

from the other
side of town
but smart enough
to leave her
sheets behind
for another's
wife to smell
and wash
with thoughts
all her own
and alone with
only soiled
sheets to have and
to hold

The Bone Yard

the bone yard
is not full of bones
human or otherwise
it is filled with
tears and failed
dreams of not
those who went
before me but
me myself
and no one else
to blame for
life's mishaps
which I accrued
like yesterday's
bank account which
never balanced
no matter how
much I tried to
be normal and
such but never
made it to the
finish line of
life but ended
up short in the
bone yard of
despair and
desperation

Rice Paddies

rice paddies
not Krispies
produced a lot more
than rice as any
Vietnam vet will
tell you so
once you slide
down the dike
and into the field
the rice
disappeared
as you waded
waist high in the
muck of a gooks
future dinner
gun held high
and ready
as can be in a
rice paddy full
of water and shit
onwards we waded
towards another
dike which would
be dry but exposed
to the enemy's
bullets and their
leeches which
covered our arms
and legs
and our lighters
and matches

were wet and would
not light to make
the leeches move
backwards and out
as only a tropical
forest vet would
know
but an extra pair
of dry socks was all
that mattered
because our feet
were never dry and
just turned white
with an ailment we
just called crud
so
welcome to the Nam
as it once was and
people long forgot
except the pain in
my dry feet did not
listen and I hobble
and sometimes regret

Some Have It

some have it
some don't and
I do not mean
a shrink
but depression
one of the cruelest
afflictions a god
ever bestowed upon
mankind or at least
part of mankind
the cruel part
I inhabit and can't
share with anyone
for it is truly an
indoor sport and
between the sheets
of an unmade bed
which will never be
made as long as the
occupant remains
depressed
I once read that
depression was a
self infliction of
the weak but
I wonder often
like alcoholism
is it my fault
sure does when I
am depressed
and a trip to

the bathroom to
brush my teeth
is as difficult
as the Marine
Corps boot camp
I endured so
many years ago
when the only
depression
I knew was an
off base weekend
hangover which
I thought was
hell in itself
but I was wrong
terribly wrong
as the first
incoming rounds
hit home and
readily killed
my buddies
but compared
to their
families I had
nothing to be
depressed about
but I soon forgot
about then
and was depressed
now
and a days
accomplishment
is turning off the

porch lights or
bringing in the
papers
and dusk is no
different from
dawn because
the blinds are
drawn tight
and my only
respite is next
weeks meeting
with my shrink
and pretending
for five days
that I am
normal
until the shrink
and I
next speak

Ode to John Belushi

John Belushi
I truly miss more
than my mother
and father
and all of the
other dead ones
in my life

he of all people
shared my agony
and never
complained but
partied on as
I was afraid

to do so and I
now sit writing about
he who had
the courage
to end it all
and depart this
world on top

of his game
from the life of
a comic apart
from the man
I would love to

have talked with
and discussed

why it was that
I am putting
a pistol in

my mouth and
drugs in his
veins but not
mine which
does not really

matter
he is a movie
and I am
merely a
poem

that no one
will read
except the
late great
John Belushi

Pig In a Blanket

pig in a blanket
is how I felt
early one morning
while camping as
a youth with
my family
it was very cold
that night
and the heat
from the campfire
wore off
hours ago
so to the bottom
of my sleeping
bag I went
seeking warmth
and fell asleep
apparently
for I awakened
breathless and
in panic
as I could not
find an exit
from the bag
in which I was
sleeping
I panicked
not finding an
exit or fresh
air but only
my brother

sitting on the
top of the bag
and keeping me
in the dark
hours after
the sun had
risen and the
campfire
started
I vowed to
kill him
as my fears
of claustrophobia
continued
throughout my
life
but maybe I
did kill him
for he
eventually
tried to kill
himself
thinking
he was me.

The Bird

the bird
sat alone in a tree
on a branch
no different
from the others

he tweeted
for a mate
but never found
one before he
remembered

what the wise
bird once said.
that once
the white man
had a gun
the little bird
could no longer
perch alone
in a tree,

because
before
it heard
the sound
its wings would
fold and it would
fall to the earth
like so many
other birds who
did not listen
to the wise bird's words

Switching Identities

switching identities
is not as hard
as you think
but you must
first make sure
that the other
identity is dead
so it becomes
a matter of
morals
can you kill him
and take his
passport while
he lays bleeding
or can you not
in which you will
be stuck with the
identity of your
birth and go
nowhere
different
but the sound
of the gun
and the burnt
power
in the air
leads me to
believe you made
the right choice
same as
in 1968

when I killed
Ernie
for the very
same reason.

Foreign Jails

foreign jails
are not that bad
and I know
very well
because I have
shit and pissed
with 200 Salvadorans
watching and not
speaking English
at least
to me
the guards are
relaxed
and the judge
is nowhere
to be found
this hot and
humid
lockup
4th of July
when no one
cared about
all of us
imprisoned
behind bars
speaking
different
languages
that said
the same thing
why am I here

and why is a
gringo among us
in a land we
thought was
free.

The Dike

the dike
was the only place
we were dry if
only for a second
to let our jungle
greens pasted to
our body
breath a bit
but back we went
in single file
with guns held
overhead
into the paddies
only to lose
a limb or two
I remember
one day watching
the LT
dry as can be
directing us
forward
into a fog
shrouded paddy
next to a 'ville
of no concern
but still we
fired first
when body counts
were victory
but some how
I survived

but with blood
on my hands
no matter how
much I wash
but I just love
being dry

<u>The Hole</u>

the hole
in my back yard
is scary
very deep
and it was
not there
before
but it beckoned
me about
my past
and the things
I did wrong
and regret
but cannot
undo to allow
me to start
over again
but the hole
grew bigger
when I thought
about my
wrongs
and how
I could not
make amends
that would
suffice
to make
the hole
smaller
and myself

less guilty
but still
the hole
beckoned.

Squirrels

squirrels
were my moms
favorite and
as she grew old
she forgot
their names
so just called
them all
squirrely

people asked
her about this
name and she
only said and
pointed with
wrinkled and
blue veined
fingers

for the
questioner
to watch them
and realize
they acted
squirrely
and all
readily agreed

in her very later
years she would
spend evenings

with my father
just off the
back porch of
their beloved
home our
childhood home

he smoking his
pipe and reading
a year old Time
magazine while
the squirrels
ran about on the
lawn chasing my
mothers peanuts

the black birds
watching from the
wires above
ready to descend
and steal the nuts
As my very practical
father predicted

but he was wrong
often when it came
to my mother and
her antics for she
had taught the
squirrels to hide
their nuts in the ivy
trailing down the
brick of our old

childhood homestead
and dad never caught
on against his German
catholic instincts as
to how mom was fooling
him with the squirrels
and the nuts

for I always believed
he favored the black
birds until his eyes
failed and through
the smoke of his pipe
he could no longer
tell a black bird
from a squirrel

and his counsel told
him it really did not
matter

A Book Thief

I once was
haunting the lairs
of dusty old
book sellers
and their
precious books
which they truly
hated to sell even
as they starved
not paying
attention to
those who walked
up and down
their aisles
that's when I
stuffed rare books
down the back
of my three piece
Brooks Brothers suit
they took no notice
not interested
in money
or financial
gain but only
to possess which
I eventually did
and displayed
all 5,000 of my
books on shelves but no one
cared it was the eighties
when coke was

more important than books
still they came
to see me
while the books
where so much
decoration
to all but an
ex-wife
who backed up
a trailer to my
gallery and
off-loaded all
books to pay her
lawyer but
not mine
so I dusted the
empty shelves
licked my wounds
and bought a
ticket to Nicaragua
where some
25 years later
books matter
again to the poor
who have never
seen a bookmobile

Pepe the Penguin

Pepe the penguin
is such a
handsome devil.

Clarke Gable
on ice awaiting
the next ball.

with his tux
continually
pressed by his
retractable
flippers

to impress
no one but
certainly
everyone in
the rookery

who now seemed
so far away
by an expanse
of water his
mother had
warned about

but how could
he watch the
ice floes when
his tuxedo

looked so good
at least to
himself alone

on the ice flow
and he had to
jump to join
the others who
waved him on
and watched
the shark eat
the tuxedo

Demons

demons
I am so very
happy now
surrounded by
darkness
having washed off
the dirt and
disdain of today's
encounters
with those
who just
did not care
as much about
me as I
did about them
did I mention
my bathrobe
not sure if I did
but winter is
upon us
the snow
covering up
the ugliness
but not the
hatred I saw
on the streets
today
where I got
my bathrobe
and soon
to grab a hot

meal with others
who are already
my very best
friends and
then some
I got my pillow
or maybe
someone else's
recycled as
so many dreams
before I lay
down my head
to face
my demons who
most likely by
morning will have
stolen my only
shoes and on a
cold and wet
Portland day
until morning
they had said
and all would
look brighter
but they lied
and I took my
pipe with me
after breakfast
when I
hit the streets

<u>My Last Poem</u>

my last poem
is something
I've wanted to tell
for a long time
it is a goodbye
of sorts
it means nothing more
than
I have given up on life
and am a failure after all
I have tried
to be better
but still I exist
going to sleep
wondering about
the downside
and
the morning
to come
which I fear
because it might be
just like
the morning before

<u>The Missionary</u>

the missionary
had a smile like Satan
for He well knew that
the world's problems and wars
were not caused by people
but a lonely and vengeful god
who had been smote by
the decrease in his minions
who no longer felt that
people caused wars
and disasters
of a proportion only a
god can do
to make them believe
in him and his wrath
and make people suffer
as the proper lady exiting
a church once said
disasters and deformed children
are gods way of making
you stronger
as his people tithe
to pay for his popes ring
while the people starve
around the world
because he says
they deserve it

<u>Neighbors</u>

neighbors
especially
in my neighborhood
where none of us
are separated
by fences
are simply
the greatest
at least tonight
they sure were
and turned my holiday
BBQ into a surprise
and belated
birthday party
whose generosity
always makes for
too much cake
which I do not eat
too much ice cream
I do not eat
and they always
try to put the garbage
under the sink
like in most homes
but not mine
so here I sit
rearranging everything
the little ones touched

and the adults
did not know
they were touching
but when I opened
the fridge
and saw all the leftovers
I smiled but not
at the amount
but their generosity
so fences
do not
necessarily
good neighbors
make
at
least
not
in my
humble
but proud
neighborhood

A Yellow Room

a yellow room
was what I requested
from my shrink
before I departed
for the asylum
no problem he said
just before they
buckled me into
my white jacket
expecting my room
to be yellow
however
because
most inmates
probably
did not care about
color
as they were buckled
drooling
and electro-shocked
without
however
my fine sense
of décor
would not accept
the pea-green
government
paint of the austere

rooms
for which others were
bound
and
blindly accepted
but not me the
experienced
decorator
who knew
just what he wanted
yellow
like all things
outside
that they wanted
me to forget
dandelions
butterflies
school buses
the sun
bumble bees
yellow sweaters
on school girls
snow yellowed
by a dog
or Van Gough's
yellow café
painting
but
of course
just about

anything
not green
as my walls
are now
when in reality
the only yellow
I ever saw
was the urine
running down
my legs
after
shock
therapy
which stayed moist
throughout
the long night
as others howled
and I thought
about tomorrow
and the yellow
sunrise
which they could
not
take away
only the winter
clouds
could do
such

The Garden Hose

the garden hose
waters the lawn
in summer
as well as
the flowers
sometimes
or maybe just
something to
spray other
kids with your
thumb on the
nozzle or to
fill squirt guns
with which to
spray the
girls
but when
it is attached
to a sprinkler
to water the
big lawn
it is very
dangerous
to jump
through it
without
dads
permission

but then
with his ok
we all run
and jump
through it
with glee
forgetting
that
summer
would soon
be over
and someday
they
would not
have a
summer
like they
once
remembered
but the hose
would
be there
hanging in
the garage
ready when
they needed
it to put
one end
into the
exhaust

pipe and
the other
end into
the mostly
closed
window
and go to
sleep
forever

A Bad Marriage

A bad marriage
is more
disorienting
than a
desert wind
just swirling
and swirling
picking up
more dust
with no
where to go
until it
dissipates
but not
forgotten
as it leaves
havoc and
destruction
in its wake
only to start
again
somewhere
else and
repeat itself
in the guise
of a second
marriage

Whale Tears

I visited the coast recently
got a cabin by the sea
on a cliff really
not on the sea
cheaper
and that counts

settled in comfort
wanted a drink
of anything
that smelled of booze
didn't imbibe
watched the sun rise

feeling much better
than if I had
gone to the kitchen
overlooking the bay
scrambled some eggs
an omelet or sorts
and wished for a drink

then
I saw the whales
surfacing in the bay
grabbed my camera
and watched them display
their nautical touch

as my breakfast burned
and I grabbed
a drink
as so many times before
and forgot about the whales
but only the ice cubes
as the whales kept surfacing
splashing about
their fins above water
as if to shout
their presence
and bigness

like the elephant
I suppose
I no longer cared
about the whales
and life
other than mine

soon they disappeared
beneath the blue deep
to surface somewhere
else
I hope
and safely to keep

I washed the dishes
looking some more
they never came back

as the water
in the sink
went down the drain

and I emptied another glass
with more to come
and sat down and cried
for the first time
remembered
not about the whales

their beauty aside
but to celebrate life
like never before
of which I knew not such
so I packed up my bag
and drove away drunk

not hitting a whale

A Weapon

a weapon
of
less
destruction
not
mass
destruction

of that
we know
too much
but
self
destruction
is
our own
choice
god
gave us
a hand
and
we build
the gun

god
did he
really
build

the
gun
and
not thee
surely we should know
my weapon is fully loaded
and both hands are free

so just pull the trigger
and remember for me
the destruction of my war
and PTSD

I was broken at birth
I did not cry
I saw a hole in the sky
that hope could not fill
at least not for me

so I remain broken
and care for myself
no family to worry about
my gun on a shelf
sitting next to a mouse

my fingers are paralyzed
as just in a dream
my intentions are clear
but I fear
I am just like the mouse

afraid to eat cheese

but the pistol awaits
in fear of no one
wanting off the shelf
to get the job done

the rooster cried
because
he was afraid
to die
as so many
before him
did such

in a chalk ring
with so many pesos
fluttering about
and feathers
with blood
lying about

he was afraid
and not of a tear
as long
as no one watched
it fall
outside

the ring
where the betting
took place
no riches for him
nor those
by his side

to be a rooster
was bad enough
but
to be a coward
in feathers
was a disgrace

Bob's Goodbye
(The Final Words of An Individual Known as Bob)

Dear Lord,
I am afraid of you
and, I do not really know if you exist
but, I do know I will never be happy
or, ever in love
so, please
do not let me be lonely
or, die alone
and, always remember
you are what I am afraid of
it is your fault
that a place called Purgatory exists
for non-baptized babies
that is why I hate you so much Lord
and why I want to fight you to the death
if we ever meet
your death will be my resurrection
not in a cave
or, from a cross
but in my soul
I will defeat you
and in the process
remove all the evils from this world
beware my elusive friend
you have met your match!

Letters

to

Bob

For the most part, the following letters have been reproduced without any editing or manipulation by the publisher. We wanted Bob to hear the words from his friends just the way each had intended.

Dear Bob,

I want to take this opportunity to thank you for being my dear friend. I met you at Swannie's Bar in Seattle and you turned my life upside down. We really got to know each other during a road trip to Kamloops, British Columbia with the Swannie's Studs Baseball team. That result of that trip was my owning the team the following year and 28 years of involvement with the team. After I got to get to know you, I realized that you had a rapport with people few others have. The following year I hired you as a salesman for my company, unfortunately you left my employment a few years later for another printing company. Even though you left at the point where I was finally making some money with you, we remained friends.

After you moved to Boulder, I had the good fortune to visit you quite a few times. The first trip you had me picked up by a limo in Denver, quite a first impression. I have wonderful memories of partying with Michael, Roxanne and yourself. I met some great folks at the bookstore, the bagel shop, and a number of eating establishment.

What I will remember you the most for are the great stories, stories that inspired my two boys and myself to never be afraid of the adventure of life. You have touched the lives of people around the world. You are the great adventurer, who has given Hemingway a run for his money.

Steve Potter

Bob!

I miss you a lot. I miss our conversations, you with your adventures, both past and present, as well as those planned, from Boulder to Bengali.

When I close my eyes and think of you, I think of our adventure in Jamaica, where we delivered shoes and books for One World Running. Or Nicaragua, or Cuba. How everywhere we went, people knew you, and loved you.

How you were so generous with your time, offering advice, and how you collected autographs. You were a giant oak tree, that drew life from all over. You remain an inspiration for many of us. Good-bye and from all of those you touched, thank you.

Blessings forever, Mike
(Michael Sandrock)

Bob,

Thanks for being such a great friend over the years. It's been over forty years since you came up to the University of Washington after your service in Vietnam with the Marines searching for some kind of path to the future and I really appreciate that we have maintained the kind of friendship that transcends time and distance.

I think one of your greatest attributes is your ability to make friends. You had a lot of them, despite your tendency to cut yourself off from them as you shifted from one phase of your life to another. It is amazing how close you can get to someone with just a short conversation in a hotel lobby on one of your many trips to the outer edges of civilization.

I remember vividly that monumental odyssey that we took together in 1969, setting out together in an old milk truck we outfitted into an early version of an SUV. On that trip, you began your transformation from a pumped-up hard-partying troglodyte to a world-wise traveler, tasteful collector, consummate "letters to the editor" writer, world traveler, impeccable interior decorator and erstwhile poet.

Through the years as our lives have grown and changed, we have managed to keep in touch even though we have been blown by the winds of change through many personal triumphs and failures. Friendship, true friendship is a rare commodity. We have it and I know it will continue despite the vagaries of life.

Your friend,
Jim "Nytro" Nystrom

Bob,

I met you in the very early 90's when I was the Head Golf Professional at Havana Golf Club, Havana, Cuba. Bob, do you remember how long we have known each other?

Let me tell you that you played a very important part in my golf career, I'm very proud to say that you are the friend that everyone would like to have in their lives. I want to thank you for all the time we have spent together, playing golf or organizing a golf tournament, talking about future projects or about a golfing day for some of your groups, or just smoking a very good cigar from my homeland. They were just great times, believe me.

Thank you so much, Bob. Take care.
Jorge Duque

Dear Bob,

We met over the phone in 1993! The former President of my country, Colombia, and my partner in a cultural TV company, introduced me to you, by fax! The telephone was our first way of building a friendship. Later, attending a TV market in San Francisco we met at the Saint Francis Hotel, of course, by the clock. You wanted to explore new projects and new people, and to find things to do. With you I discovered the best hamburgers in San Francisco.

We continued talking, planning, and imagining a business. In 1994, came your Cuban adventure, experience, romance? And I met there, some of my very good friends that day. Cuba days, the doctors, the visits to the hospitals, meeting architect Mario Coyula and La Habana scale model, the young sports people you wanted to help, the Foreign Affairs Minister, conferences....Ernest Hemingway Marlin Tournament, meeting Gregorio Fuentes and school kids in Cojimar. At the end of that year, the Denver - Boulder group got together at a friend's house and enjoyed it all together. I flew in from Colombia. Same in 1996, 1998.

In 1999 I moved to Spain as a diplomat, but the phone kept us connected. And the Hemingway love affair with Spain nourished our calls: bullfights, Pamplona, Seville.

I listened, I knew, Costa Rica, Nicaragua, India, Pakistan, Afghanistan, all the help you wanted to give all over, and always to Cuba. Your accidents, your sicknesses.....Until 2011.

It was worth being awakened in the middle of the night! You weren't good with the time difference!

Your friend,
Adriana Dominquez Navia

Dear Bob,

I wonder if you knew how much you meant to those of us who grew up with you in Vancouver. I know how much you meant to those of us who went to school with you. I know how much you meant to those of us who palled around with your sisters Judy, Jean and Jo. I know how much you meant to those of us whose parents were great friends with your mom and dad. But, did you know?

When you walked into a room, you owned it. Your presence was commanding. You were handsome. You were entertaining. You were smart. You were inspirational. You were nurturing. You were hilarious. And sometimes you seemed a little bit scary, but I always thought you meant to seem so.

I'll always remember your laugh and your smile and your voice and the twinkle in your eye - and the stories, oh, the stories you told - and be glad that I was lucky enough to have known you.

Did you know how much we would miss you?

Robin McMullen Hanna

Hi Bob:

I wish wherever you are that you have found the peace you never had. I will always remember the good moments we had in Havana between "mojitos" and "cigars" during the many years we spent together. Your great heart will always be remembered by all your Cuban friends, rest in peace **mi amigo**.

Adios,
Jose I. Fuentes
Havana, Cuba

Bob,

I miss your booming voice, your adventurous spirit, and your generous heart. I miss your monthly phone calls and your exciting stories. I miss sharing the "latest" Bob Walz story with my wife, and watching her stare at me in amazement, as if nobody could actually experience those things......but you did. You lived the life that most people only dream about, and you were able to share it with your friends.

Thank you for introducing me to Cuba. Thanks for making sure I was safe, and that my trip was organized. Thanks for showing me places I always wanted to see.....places that most people never get to see. Thanks for introducing me to your friends and colleagues, whom are now my friends. Thanks for introducing me to your mother, and allowing me the honor of having dinner with her on a special night in Havana. Thanks for being so generous and selfless, always looking out for others. Thanks for always asking about my wife, my dogs, my family – even though you were suffering and should be consumed with yourself.

Thanks for your friendship Robert Henry Walz. Ten years was not enough, but I hope to catch up with you someday at Club 21 in heaven.

Colin Stuart Weeks

Dear Bob

   We shared so many things together. Starting at Providence Academy where we began our formal education with the Sisters of Charity. Boy were they in for a shock before we left. Remember coming home from school one day and finding this "KOTEX" machine abandoned in the woods. We brought it home knowing there would be some sort of reward for this sophisticated piece of equipment that must of fallen out of a military plane. We couldn't figure out why my mom was laughing so hard when we finally arrived at my house (of course we opened it up to inspect the contents). You always one-up me, this time by safety pining two badges of honor around your head when I only had one. And you made me salute you. Remember when we raced home in the middle of the October 12th day wind storm? Even though the wind gusts were up to 100 mph, you decided to take a short cut through Luko's apple orchard to beat me. Yes, you won, but you looked like someone dipped you in a bowl of black and blue apple sauce. You beat me home again my friend!!!!!! I miss you terribly.

Roger Ehle

Roses in a Box

One October day, which happened to be my 23rd Birthday, a boy entered Signature's gallery with a long silver box. You cannot imagine the fluttering of my heart when the boy announced that it was for me! I laid the box on my little wooden desk and lifted the top. There were six at one end and six at the other, their long thin stems touching at center, a dozen of the most perfect yellow roses I had ever seen. The card inside, a treasure still pressed in my scrap book, reads simply: "A beautiful thing deserves beautiful things. Happy Birthday Beautiful, Bob."

What was most precious to me was that these were not roses from a suitor or a lover but from a someone whose friendship, for decades to come, would remain steadfast, never waning. I hope that over the years I was able to show him how much I loved him by always picking up the telephone when he called during every lonely hour... By laughing at his hilarious sense of humor, by praising his brilliance, and by reminding him how wonderful he was when he was troubled by doubt and insecurity.

I hope I told him enough how much I loved him, and that in his final hours he may have thought of me, remembering, and smiled.

I will miss him all the days of my life.

Kathleen (Huizar) Ledoux

Well, congrats Uncle Buck on getting your stories and poems published. A special thanks to Val for all his help. I think about you every day and have grown to miss the late night calls to discuss nothing and everything. You were the best uncle I could have asked for: teaching me swear words, showing me pictures of naked women, shooting birds with pellet guns, and always getting your nephews to test the boundaries of mischief.

I wanted to thank you for your service to this country and always admired your desire to help those who served. Thank you for always expressing interest in my professional and personal life and giving me confidence to pursue my dreams and become a better person. You were a great listener and even better bull shitter. Your generosity was second to none, and your ability to go out of your way to make people feel good is something everyone should strive for in life.

You caused me lots of tears and laughs Bob, and I will always have our memories together. I hope to see you again someday and hear about the score you settled with God. In your words, May the wind always be at your back. Safe travels amigo.

Best,
Jimmy

Hey you, I think of you every night, sometimes twice, when I turn my pillow over to the cool side. Bob, remember when we were talking about how that was something we both liked? Strange habit.

When I came to visit you in October 2011, I never thought it would be the last time I would see you and that just two weeks later you would be gone from this world.

It was during that visit and the prior 6 months that we had rekindled our 27-year friendship. It was wonderful hearing the stories and experiences of your remarkable life and we had some good laughs didn't we? I will always cherish those two days - I fixed your broken bookcase (you were in such awe), you loved the orange Chinese lanterns from my garden, and I got to see your incredible art works. I bought a painting and you gave me a few things. You called it your pre-posthumous sale but I thought you were making room for more art. Those things that were yours have a place of honor in my home and every time I look at the Hindu dancing girl, or the Copacabana Hotel plate, now on my kitchen wall, or the girl on the train painting, I say aloud a little under my breath, "Oh Bob." When we said our goodbyes that last day of our visit, as you walked away I knew you were crying a little and I was too.

Norene Sandifer

Dear Hermano Bob,

I'm not sure where to begin expressing my gratitude to you. From our first trip to Cuba in the early 90s to my 3rd trip in 1998, I've learned that living life to the absolute last drop fullest does not have to be wishful thinking. It can be done, because you did it. And helped inspire so many others to do the same.

My parents and their friends from the Gulf Coast and New Orleans asked about you for years following that memorable '98 trip, where I got engaged (ok, so the marriage didn't last, but the fond memories do). They loved you as I knew they would. The way you could talk to them with such ease and humor, the way you patiently responded to the barrage of questions as if it was the first time anyone had asked you those.

You even came to my wedding which was an honor. And one of our last good communications came right after the BP Oil spill disaster. Being fresh back from your volunteer trip to Haiti, you offered to go down to Ms and help out our friends. You're a kind, giving soul, amigo, with the enthusiasm of eternal youth to go along with it.

I know you'll run into my Dad up there, another never-met-a-stranger world traveler who so enjoyed your company, so please give him a hug for me.

You're missed and loved, my friend.

Will Robinson

Bob:

I want to thank you for all the great times we had together from high school through the University of Washington, while in California, Colorado, and Washington. I thoroughly enjoyed your whole family. This includes your father, a family practitioner, your mother, a nurse and former President of the National Red Cross and your four siblings. You were a joy to be around. Your glass was always half full while going through life. Your memories will live on. God bless the man that was not always right but never in doubt. May your rest in peace.

Gregory Zoller, M.D.

Dear Bob,

I miss you! As long as I can remember, being with you was an adventure. You could make anyone feel good and accepted and you seemed relaxed in any situation and within minutes even a stranger had become a friend.

You were always so interested in what I did and you were an incredibly supportive uncle to my sons. I remember so many great times: just hanging in the living room at 4900 Cherry Street or in Seattle at Earl's or your gallery or our trip to LA with the boys and driving around Ireland with you or throwing rocks at the Lewis River or your trip to Richmond and shooting bb guns at Mt. Hood and Mr. Fliberty Jibbit and so many, many other times.

It was the stories, always a story. The line between reality and BS was blurred but once I accepted that, it was much more fun to be with you. I know you thought you were hiding your real self from the world, but we knew you and loved you anyway.

A big thank you to Val who always believed in you and who made this book happen. Your spirit and love of life live on in our memories and now in your words. I know that you are finally at peace with those you love and those who love you. I love you and miss you so much,

Your little sister,
Judy

Dear Bob,

Your professional approach and committed to work are major factors in ensuring high standards of personnel achievement. These qualities have brought about a high degree of respect from all who associated with Bob.

As a colleague you were one of the most efficient and capable I have had. As a friend you were one who was always willing to listen and lend a hand if I needed it. Bob was optimistic and genuine in his behavior with people.

Dear Bob, I keep in mind your advice that most change happens in small steps and every action we take will count towards the overall creating of a new world.

On behalf of the local village students and nature guide of the Bandhavgarh and Corbett Tiger Reserve, I want to express my sincere thanks for the opportunity to enhance our library's book collection.

I admire very much your spirit, and your expression of love and commitment towards conservation and education are most meaningful.

Sincerely,
Ajay Ghale
Chief Naturalist & Naturalist Training
Syna Tiger Resort
Bandhavgarh National Park & Tiger Reserve
Tala Bandhavgarh,Dt.Umaria,Madhya Pradesh,
Pin:484661
India

Dear Bob,

I know I don't say it enough, so I wanted to make an opportunity to thank you for your friendship. From meeting you in Boulder in 1998 and co-operating the first (legal) Eco-adventure in Cuba a few years later to moving (back) to the Pacific Northwest at the same time and having numerous lively conversations about how to mainstream the concept of sustainable tourism in the travel sector, I value the rich experiences and rich dialogue we've shared. Your unrelenting enthusiasm for life, infectious personality, strong entrepreneurial spirit, and fascinating travel tales have made a deep impression on me. Thank you for being you and for positively impacting so many wonderful people throughout your life.

With all my best,

Brian Mullis

Dear Bob,

THANK YOU. Thank you being a great client and a wonderful friend. Thank you for giving me the opportunity to organize your mom's 85th birthday party here in Cancun. I will always remember how we met and the great pleasure we had together with your clients, our dinners at the bullring, along with your wonderful stories. I will remember all our chats, all the wonderful people I have met because of you, and introducing me to my big brother, Val. Thank you for everything, for your support, your kindness, your words and consideration, most of all for giving me the opportunity to be part of your life.

There are so many stories to tell and each makes me laugh. I remember when you and Val stopped by my house and took Ricardo, my former husband, to God knows where. He came home drunk, but very happy. I remember I gave you the last present, a Mayan figure, to be placed in your house. We felt proud to have something in your house made exclusively for you.

When my former boss at Hyatt asked me to take care of your account, I was very nervous, but excited! You made that transition very easy. When I moved to another hotel, you followed me, teaching me that you made business with people, not companies.

You never knew this, but the bellboys at the Hyatt wouldn't speak to me for almost a year because you left the hotel. They, too, said you were a splendid man and indeed you are, wherever you are, I LOVE U.

With Love,
Silvia Gutierrez

Ghosts

ghosts
wrench us at night
repeat their tale
until each line is perfectly said
our subterranean selves
undisturbed by our superficial selves
busy effective successful
the external life that we don't
quite attend to
as we track the haunted tale
currently running
in the mind we conceal
that rules our lives

rules
until we speak to it
speak it to the outer world
then we find the light
the road that delivers us
to peace
acceptance
ourselves

this voice
your own
expressing the terrors within
this voice
releases us from fear
oh Bob
you found the road
at last at last
expressed the shock
the sorrow
that crushes us
when we learn
by living it
what humans can do
when they live in
love and respect
the catharsis
of community

Jim Martin

Bob,

"IT'S NOT THE YEARS THAT COUNT,
IT'S THE MILES!"

Vios con Dios

Semper Fi

Anon.

Cousin Bob Walz, everybody's friend.

What a guy of many talents and a particularly great story teller. You never let the FACTS get in the way of a good story. We had many good times starting with camping trips as kids to Swan Lake in central Washington. Touch football in your back yard was fun until you got too big for us to handle. Also remember the drag races on the Lower River Road when Nordy's hot rod raced against Evelyn's (my mother) 1957 Ford. No wonder the transmission went out at 29,000 miles. Finally, your return to Vancouver to help your parents in their later years was very thoughtful. We enjoyed every time we met as something was always new. We miss you pal.

Bill Cone

Bob,

You were always the fun one, never a dull moment. Always full of piss and vinegar with a heart of gold. You transported me to wonderful countries through your adventures—and they were adventures!! We never knew if your tales were 100% correct or 10% correct and 90% bs.

Missing you,
Your favorite cousin—MA.

Bob,

While I have been coming to grips with your passing, and glad that you're out of a rapidly failing body, I still find your absence to be a grievous process. Recalling conversations, shared experiences, images and, of course, the laughter with you, Walzie, (as I most often addressed you), it made me realize how special you were.

The times you would call to talk about current events, your travels, or just to talk, were always welcomed. They were filled with quick wit, insight, and humor. I miss not being able to give you a quick call. You called me one day before your passing and reminded me of a time we drove up to a mountain stream and sat on some rocks to smoke cigars and converse. I felt lucky to be in your inner circle.

We worked out together for many years, which gave me a chance to spend a lot of quality time with you. During that time, I watched you reinvent yourself and do what you loved to do most; travel, and create adventures for yourself and others. You had an amazing ability to ingratiate yourself to people. You were warm, full of life, and interesting. Most people loved you right off the bat. You loved your Mom and Dad above all, and saw them any chance you could get. You also loved to read, write, smoke cigars, and drink your Vodka. (I always thought you had a little Ernest Hemingway in you.)

"Here's to you" my good old friend. I celebrate you and your life. You are forever memorialized in my heart and mind. Maybe we can meet up again sometime.

Stu Kanter

Dear Bob,

Been anywhere interesting lately? I heard you were on another great adventure! I remember you taking me under your wing here and there, like when I first met you in Cuba, way beyond the cigar factories and the incredible fishing—I remember the thrill of meeting Castro; the intrigue leading up to my interview with him and the barter involving those Cuban missile crisis aerial photos with JFK's handwritten notes; the access to Comandante Guillermo Garcia with his family and his letting me ride his magnificent stallion—to this day the finest horse this Texan has ever ridden; smoking cigars with Hemingway's friend...old man what's-his-name...yeah, *that* one, from the Old Man and the Sea, Gregorio Fuentes; and in meeting Gregorio how we went by the home of Jose's friend and saw the young boy who was playing baseball at the neighborhood diamond with the cardboard glove he had made. There's so much that it became a blur—the cock fights, the Pinar Valley, the tobacco farmer and his mule-drawn plow in the Pinar Valley. Hmmm, did I hear that Gregorio was with you on this new adventure of yours? If so, tell him hi.

Speaking of adventure, I remember ours in Nicaragua, being able to go into the territory forbidden to any people other than the Rama Indians, as a result of the access you had secured, looking for their Lost City in the dense jungle. But my most vivid memories with you there were intensely personal, when we maneuvered that honey-colored stream with primeval trees fallen into the water and dappled —the stuff of boyhood dreams—to find the last shaman of those Rama Indians. You, with your cancer and me with my friend Bob, seeking answers. What a story, the gathering of rare plants from his jungle garden and the rain forest itself, the day-long hunt for that one must-have root—maybe the last of its kind, the making of the tea itself in the shaman's open-air thatched-roof dwelling. The remission of your cancer.

Man o man, I wish we could bottle that stuff. Well, I guess we actually did—bottle it, that is—smuggling liters of it into the country. I wish there had been more where that came from, for later.

I remember all of our trips together, but I won't include those that are too nefarious in this letter. It might fall into the wrong hands! You never know who might end up reading this! But you know, old friend, as much as I thank you for such memories, I want you to know it's been your displays of generosity and thoughtfulness that I've most admired. When we went back to that little home in Cuba where the boy had been playing baseball with the cardboard glove he had fashioned, you made certain we took him a leather fielder's glove. And I remember too, when the shaman would not take money, you made certain we took him a pig.

Come to think of it, I heard the shaman was bitten by a pit viper. I hope he made it through. For some reason, I think he too might be with you on your new adventure. So tell him hi for me as well. The same goes for all the other old characters we befriended—the shaman, Gregorio, the ex-head of the KGB in the Eastern Block (what was his name?), the Rhode Island mafia (hi boys!), and on and on—tell them all hi if they're with you on your new adventure. I heard it was crossing some big river, with some incredible treasure on the other side.

Your buddy, Steve Connatser

SUE BEAR,

WALZY LEAVES BEHIND MANY FRIENDS ALL OVER THE WORLD! WE ALL FEEL LUCKY TO HAVE KNOWN HIM!

I KNOW BOB WROTE THIS BOOK, BECAUSE I DID NOT UNDERSTAND HALF OF IT. HA, HA,

I KNOW HE LOVED US, AS WE LOVED HIM.

WELL, LOVE-YA SUE-BEAR, THIS IS ALL WE GOT LEFT OF OUR TRUE BROTHER,

P.S. HE WAS OUR FAMILY

LOVE, YOUR BRO.

1246303R00255

12-12-12

Made in the USA
San Bernardino, CA
05 December 2012